THE WRITING TEACHER'S COMPANION

THE WRITING TEACHER'S COMPANION

Planning, Teaching, and Evaluating in the Composition Classroom

Rai Peterson
Ball State University

HOUGHTON MIFFLIN COMPANY   BOSTON   TORONTO
Geneva, Illinois   Palo Alto   Princeton, New Jersey

Sponsoring Editor: George Kane
Senior Associate Editor: Melody Davies
Production Coordinator: LuAnn Belmonte Paladino

Printed in the U.S.A.

ISBN: 0-395-35033-6

3456789-B-99 98

Contents

PART THREE CLASSROOM MANAGEMENT 95

PART FOUR TEXTBOOKS

Foreword

The first time I entered a freshman composition classroom, I was the teacher. That is the all-too-common experience of many of us who teach writing. Convinced to major in English in college because of innate skills, we are exempted from general education requirements in our chosen field. As graduate students or recent M.A.s, we receive the assignment for which we have waited: to organize, present, and evaluate a college class, using the best of what we have observed in our own teachers and the insights we have gleaned from teacher education (psychology, research review, or history of the discipline courses). Most of us are quick to discover that fragments of good pedagogy and individual exciting assignments, although promising, do not provide solid theoretical bases or long-term course objectives.

Besieged by doubt, I wondered on the eve of my debut as a classroom teacher whether writing could even be *taught*. Although I vividly recalled grade school phonics and seventh- and eighth-grade sentence diagramming, I could not remember ever *learning* to write. Sentences, it seemed to me, had always formed themselves, springing into my consciousness faster than I could record them with random pencil or pen. How, I wondered, could I translate innate ability into individual, sequential skills?

Fortunately, the problems inherent in teaching others to formulate, organize, and record thoughts need not be solved by every individual writing instructor. Composition instruction is an evolving body of theories and practices that readily apply to every classroom situation—from basic to advanced composition classes and from narrative to expository prose. As you implement these standard practices, you will find yourself fine-tuning assignments or discovering connections between theorists and theoretical approaches to the discipline. Although instruction in rhetoric has a long history, dating from before Aristotle, it is also changing with new technologies and complicated rhetorical situations. Writing instructors have the opportunity to test theory and to adapt and add to that body of knowledge with wisdom gained through practical experience.

This book is designed to help you organize, assess, and manage college composition classes. A lot of difficult decisions accompany the beginning of a new term. The course level you are assigned, the books you choose, the assignments you decide upon, the grading scale you specify, even the attendance policy you state—all have a quarter- or semester-long effect on the practices and methods that characterize your course. Read this book through before you commit yourself to a theoretical base or to specific course policies; it offers advice like that you might hear from experienced fellow teachers down the hallway. If you choose to adopt the suggestions offered here, you will still have latitude for customizing your own classes.

Teaching composition has proved to me that writing, indeed, can be taught. The improvement evidenced continually in student essays is formidable proof that composition theorists are on the right track and that individual assignments produce results. Perhaps the best evidence that producing clear compositions is a teachable and learnable skill is the improvement I have seen in my own writing since I began teaching. Making the writing process manifest for students has caused me to see it much more clearly than I did when words "just came to me." Elusive concepts such as clarity, organization, development, description, persuasion, connotation, imagery, and pacing are made explicit in the composition classroom. Recognizing that writing is a *process* implies that it is a skill to be practiced, honed, and perfected.

If you are interested and enthusiastic about writing and are willing to learn when you step up to the chalkboard on the first day of any composition class, you will be more qualified to lead it than you might suppose. During my first semesters of teaching, I depended heavily on the textbooks I had chosen for course structure, class discussion, and writing assignments. Having grown up with a passable facility with grammar, punctuation, and diction, I was technically uneducated (a result of my own boredom and laziness) about pronouns, adverbs, clauses, phrases, and so on. I managed to stay a few pages ahead of the students in the rhetoric, grammar handbook, and reader I had chosen for the course. Occasionally, I admitted to a student, "I don't know what's wrong here, but it just doesn't sound right." Then I delved into the books for the words and concepts I needed to explain the problem more clearly. Teaching myself to teach my students has taught me as much or more about writing than might have supplied by all of the instruction I previously lacked.

Whenever a student remarks (in awe or frustration), "You know all the rules," I remember myself as a graduate student hunched over the table in my kitchenette, testing myself over "who" and "whom" or some similarly sticky concept. Perhaps the truly great writers who inspire civilizations are born to their achievements, but competent writers, such as most of us and our students, are trained every day—in classrooms like yours and mine. You can teach your students to write better for themselves, their coursework, and their lives' work.

Every time you step into the classroom, your vision for your course matters more than your experience with past writing instruction. This book examines how to develop as a practitioner in a very scholarly and long-established field. The methods you, as a professional composition instructor, choose will shape not only the writing education of your immediate students but also your practice of teaching, which is essential to the field of composition.

Acknowledgments

Thank you to the following people, whose willingness to consult on the contents of this text has deepened my respect for them as scholars and teachers: Linda Hanson, Bill Holbrook, Mike Munley, Webster Newbold, Carol Papper, Paul Ranieri, Becky Rickly, Barbara Stedman, Karen Taylor, Joe Trimmer, Barbara Weaver, Patti White, and the students in Ball State University's English 610 class. Also thanks to Melody Davies, senior associate editor at Houghton Mifflin, whose ability to sail a canoe is just one testament to her resourcefulness and ingenuity. Finally, my thanks to the following instructors, who reviewed this book during its development: James E. Barcus at Baylor University, David J. Klooster at John Carroll University, Patricia A. Malinowski at Finger Lakes Community College, and Irene Patterson Ward at Kansas State University.

PART ONE

ORGANIZATION

CHAPTER 1

Basic Course Plans

WRITING-BASED CURRICULUM

Every course in a college or university curriculum is defined by its objectives, the specific content or skills instructors are hired to present and students are expected to achieve. In content-centered courses, such as literature, history, or chemistry classes, the objectives are fairly straightforward. Students learn a prescribed body of materials, usually printed in a textbook and augmented by lecture. We are all graduates of courses in which we learned, for instance, the accepted canon of American literature from 1860 through last Tuesday, or the heroic events in the history of Western civilization, or the periodic table of elements and the chemical composition of water, table salt, and an atomic bomb. Such courses are, of course, challenging to teach and study. Their content can be clearly stated from the first day, and progress toward meeting course goals can be measured objectively and monitored easily. The organization of such courses is often chronological or sequential, relying on established practice and traditional methods of purveying information and testing its acquisition.

Composition is a "contentless" course. The objective of writing classes is to build skills, not simply to communicate black-and-white information. Developing the abilities to organize ideas, elaborate descriptively, or think critically is a gradual process. Most skills can be taught by a variety of methods. Some of us learned to cook, for instance, at the elbow of a patient grandmother who taught us to measure flour and shortening by feel. Others read cookbooks and gradually branched out into experiments on our own. Still others of us look at the microwave directions on prepackaged dinners (when we remember not to discard the box too hastily). Nevertheless, most of us can produce some passable fare. Writing, like the other skills we learn, can be successfully mastered through a variety of exercises and lessons.

Successful composition classes employ a writing-based curriculum, which means the content or focus of the course is text: how it is invented, how it is organized, how it addresses its specific audience, how it makes meaning, and so on. Most writing teachers strike a balance between two kinds of text examined in class: student writing and professional models. The degree of emphasis and the methods for studying student writing, as well as the type of prose models and assignments issued, determine the focus and character of the course.

Once you decide which kinds of texts your course will emphasize, you can arrange a developmental sequence of writing assignments, or prompts, designed to practice the skills required for each type. Most courses, for example, begin with the study of personal writing (e.g., narration or story telling) and progress toward expository prose (e.g., persuasion or reporting on research). As the proposed texts for your course begin to take shape in your mind, various assignments and activities probably will occur to you as well. You are beginning to answer that most crucial of all questions in planning a college course: What, exactly, will I teach?

There are many different theories, methods, and materials available to help you organize and focus the content of the class you will teach. This chapter offers several alternatives. Perhaps one will seem eminently logical and useful, or maybe parts of each will be attractive. Most can be used in conjunction with others. The important thing to remember is that your course should be sequential, that is, each assignment should build on the skills students practiced in previous assignments. A writing course generally affords only one academic term in which to hone abilities necessary for a lifetime of productivity, and developmentally arranged tasks provide a better framework for learning than does a series of unrelated assignments.

The Writing-Process Model

Historically, writing has enjoyed a rather obscure, romantic reputation. Literature was thought to spring from the Muse full blown or was recorded verbatim from the "music of the spheres." Monarchies and papacies awarded all kinds of monetary and creature sustenance to writers, believing them to possess superior sensibilities, touched by the hand, mind, or perhaps imagination of the godhead. Some of our students still exhibit tendencies toward this sort of archaic belief. "I'm just not a writer," they will confess with undue resignation, as if learning composition were as impossible as adding six inches to their height or growing naturally red hair. (The corollary is the occasional student who insists that due dates hamper his or her innate creativity. Shake your head sadly and remind the artiste of your policy regarding late work.)

Fortunately, we live and work in the pragmatic age that has invented computer technology, space travel, the Post-it Note, and the process-based approach to teaching composition. Fundamental to the process method are two tenets: First, writing is a legitimate process that can be broken into a series of teachable skills, and second, a completed discourse or finished piece of writing does not necessarily reveal the method by which it was constructed. A composition class that emphasizes the writing process focuses on the examination of texts in various stages of completion. To this end, some textbooks include drafts or even working notes or outlines of the professional prose models they reprint. It always seems to be helpful to students to discover that all writers, even professionals and perhaps even their teachers, are not content to settle with the first draft of their work. I often show students the most cut-up, pasted-up, bruised-up drafts of my own writing in an attempt to dispel that "staying in from recess to recopy" stigma that seems to accompany the assignment of redrafting work.

Obviously the most readily available source of unfinished writing in a process-centered composition classroom is student work itself. You can make this work available to all members of your class in a variety of ways: by asking students to bring multiple copies of drafts to class on the day their work will be discussed, by copying the work yourself on your department's photocopier, or by displaying the student's copy of the paper with an overhead projector or on networked computers.

Discussing student drafts in class requires some sensitivity and skill. It takes practice to ask the kinds of open-ended questions that elicit honest comments from the class. It also is hard at first to avoid appropriating the students' text or writing process—that is, to avoid taking over and prescribing specific revisions yourself—especially since you will come up with ideas faster than the students will in your initial meetings. Class discussion of student writing should involve as many of the class members as possible, and it should present the student writer with more ideas and options than your private feedback alone would generate. Guard against letting yourself turn the classroom workshop into your own forum or a synonym for marking the draft privately. If your students feel excluded from or inferior to the process, they will quickly drop out of it, and convincing them to rejoin the discussion will be difficult.

One way to approach classroom analysis of student writing is through description of the draft under discussion. Try to avoid eliciting openly qualitative judgments about the text, which would follow if you asked questions such as, "Is the introduction complete?" or "Does this draft hold your interest?" Instead, you might ask students to outline or describe the draft. Explain that a text-in-process sometimes emphasizes material that differs from the message its writer intends to deliver, or that it may omit crucial information the writer's audience requires. Ask such questions as,

"What do you think is the main message of this piece?" or "Can you cite an example used in this draft to show specifically what the author is against?" Once descriptive analysis of the draft is under way, suggestions will start to slip in. Someone may think of a clearer way to state the thesis, or a stronger example; at that point, suggestions for revisions will be offered in a spirit of cooperation rather than as judgments.

You will quickly discover that students bring a variety of denotative and connotative definitions of *revision* to college. The first time you assign revision or a second draft you should be very explicit about what you are requiring and why. Many students automatically interpret a revision assignment as punishment, fearing they are being accused of not adequately completing the original assignment. Some will be frustrated, certain there is nothing they can add to their original response. Others will see it as busy-work, an unnecessary repetition of the same composition task. Similarly, students will have different concepts of the work involved in revision, ranging from proofreading or copyediting to blindly trying again to produce "what the teacher wants." College students are capable of appreciating the pedagogy behind assignments, so it is a good idea to offer them a brief sketch of the process approach, as well as asking them to focus on a specific skill (i.e., description) in their revisions. Your teaching will be more effective if you elicit their informed cooperation in your teaching methods.

You might ask students to consider the word *revision*, which is very much like "re-see." The first time I ask students to revise their papers, I suggest that they "re-see" not the words and sentences and problems and triumphs of the first draft but the topic or writing situation that *prompted* the first draft. I ask them to take the opportunity to see their topic or situation again, incorporating that new vision with the best of the old. If you take this approach, emphasize that they should not try to "fix" or "transform" the old text. Encourage your students to think of revision as an opportunity—not a technical or laborious task. It should be more fun than inventing the first draft because they are free to explore familiar yet unknown territory.

The process approach to teaching composition has been very influential in the field of writing pedagogy; nearly every progressive writing program incorporates some of its philosophy. It is readily adapted to other methods of course organization and writing curricula, and it is therefore a method with which you will probably want to experiment.

Modes

Every year when Charles Schultz's cartoon character Charlie Brown goes back to school, his teachers ask for the same assignment, and poor Charlie struggles dutifully to compose an essay on "What I Did During Summer Vacation." Sometimes his stilted responses are pure fantasy (an implausible adventure), occasionally they are truthful (hence boring), and in some years they border on the metaphysical (usually construed as inappropriate to the assignment). Frustrated, defeated before he begins, Charlie never seems to find the right way to relate his own experience. Meanwhile, his dog Snoopy balances a typewriter on the ridge of his doghouse and cranks out one Gothic novel after another, always starting with the first line, "It was a dark and stormy night . . . ."

The differences between the productivity of Charlie and his canine best friend are partly attributable to audience; after all, Charlie writes for a teacher, who, like all adults in the cartoon, speaks in indecipherable but clearly disapproving gibberish, while Snoopy imagines a throng of adoring fans. But equally important to their writing situations are the assignments boy and dog try to fulfill. Charlie's assignment is too specific, too narrow for a writer who has no true adventure to relate about his summer vacation. Snoopy, however, has the latitude of an entire genre in which to invent material. Having learned to compose one Gothic romance, he is inspired to write endless variations of the format.

Assignments that are too narrow (such as, "Write about a summer vacation, proudest moment, most embarrassing situation, most frightening occurrence, . . . ") may produce some fine writing among those students who can readily recall such a story-perfect experience. For the majority of student writers, however, such specific prompts elicit contrived, undeveloped prose or hopeless resignation. The problem for writing instructors, then, is twofold. Prompts must be broad enough to give students the latitude to customize the assignment. But they must also include specific parameters that define the assignment so students will know what is expected of their essays and so classroom discussions and lessons will be relevant to all students' work in progress. A modes-based approach to composition teaching provides such a workable structure for class assignments and instruction.

Modes-based instruction is derived largely from the work of nineteenth-century Scottish rhetorician Alexander Bain, who pioneered early work on paragraph structure and helped to influence, among other things, our current emphasis on the topic sentence. Bain classified the various kinds of writing by rhetorical context (audience, purpose, and organizational pattern), identifying four basic "modes" of discourse: narration, description, exposition, and argumentation. Generally, a modes-based course preserves Bain's hierarchy of types, moving from introspective writing to more expository and formally logical discourse. Modern textbooks improve on Bain's work by identifying additional modes (including process analysis, comparison-contrast, division and classification, and causal analysis), which lend more flexibility and depth to the modes-based curriculum.

Modes assignments, such as "Write an essay comparing and contrasting two seemingly similar or dissimilar topics," provide students with an open choice of specific subject matter. A student with an interest in popular music, for instance, might choose to distinguish between punk and thrash bands in her paper, while another writer, who has become very interested in an introductory architecture course, might compare ancient Greek and Mesopotamian designs for community gathering spaces. Although these topics are very different, both writers would be practicing the same principles of rhetorical organization, critical thinking, development, and awareness of audience.

The pedagogical theory behind modes-based composition instruction is that, rather than helping students hone an essay on a particular topic, it invites student writers to generalize among discourse types, practicing and improving basic communication skills. By making the rhetorical situation explicit, modes instruction helps students recognize similar situations in other contexts. For instance, students with experience writing in the comparison-contrast mode could call on that expertise in another context—if they were asked to discuss, for example, medieval French and Italian painting or gasoline versus diesel engines. A composition class organized around a sequence of modes invites students to see the "big picture," using skills acquired in early writings to develop later ones, and to recognize that those are not isolated, academic exercises but are the fundamentals of "real-life" rhetorical abilities.

Modes instruction provides at least two unique avenues of subject matter for your class meetings. Although your students will be writing about radically different topics, the general form of their work will be the same. Thus, you can focus classroom lessons and discussion on methods of development and organization common to all papers in progress. For example, if students are writing descriptive papers about topics ranging from a battlefield in a Middle Eastern desert to a basketful of newborn kittens, you might focus an in-class exercise on brainstorming details corresponding to all five senses. In both examples, details of sight, hearing, touch, smell, and maybe even taste would add to the evocative imagery of the discourse. (Incidentally, beginning writers tend to concentrate most of their descriptive details on visual imagery, so you can help your students develop their work exponentially by reminding them to draw on their other senses as well.)

Another variety of course content generated by a modes-based curriculum centers on the use of prose models. Composition anthologies, or readers, organized by modes provide students with examples of professional (and sometimes student) writing that demonstrate the rhetorical structures specified by essay assignments. These exemplify the relevant use of modes in various kinds of discourse situations, such as news reporting, personal essays, public speeches, and professional reports. Discussion of prose models encourages students to observe how professional writers develop their ideas, organize their essays, and relate to various general and specific or hostile and supportive audiences. Classroom discussions can make explicit the connections between what students are asked to read and what they are expected to write. The same principles that make a professional essay sound, publishable material make a student paper a successful response to an assignment.

Classroom discussion of prose models is easily side-tracked onto debate of the subject matter of the professional essay under examination. Such conversation is not immediately applicable to composition instruction, but it is relevant to choosing and developing topics and to a discussion of the writer-audience dynamic. Try to use students' personal responses to essays in the reader to start a dialogue about the writing itself or to maintain open channels of communication in the classroom. A few minutes' debate about George Orwell's opinion of colonialism is well spent if it heightens students' understanding of "Shooting an Elephant" and the audience for which it was originally intended. Most of us who teach writing have been strongly influenced by our reading, and you can probably remember many powerful texts that moved you to take up a pencil and respond to or imitate what you had just read. Discussion of prose models often has a similar effect on student writers, suggesting specific topics as reactions or imitations inspired by assigned readings.

In its use of prose models, modes-based writing instruction often tends to emphasize the finished essay more than does the strict process approach. In modes-based instruction process generally must be extrapolated, by guess and conjecture, from the polished prose model that appears in the textbook. However, it is far more expedient to show students clear-cut examples of process analysis, for instance, than to explain it abstractly and wait for a series of revisions to produce the optimum organizational-developmental structure. Revision can easily be incorporated in the modes-centered composition class, nonetheless. Composition instructors often encourage students to use prose models and class discussion of basic mode traits to govern the production of first drafts of an essay; they then rely on process-approach techniques to guide revisions. Modes-based composition instruction provides a strong framework for organizing course syllabi and individual lesson plans, but it is also a very flexible design that is easy to customize and adapt to individual instructors, classes, and students. For instance, it is possible to combine some conventional modes (e.g., narration-description or causal analysis-argument). You might design your course around four to eight modes, depending on such combinations, the amount of revision you plan to require, and the elements of other approaches you wish to incorporate. However you adapt it, Alexander Bain's basic approach remains a proven and very workable method of organizing the modern composition class.

Writing Across the Curriculum

My great-grandfather, when I knew him, was retired, but he kept all his carpentry tools neatly arranged in a shed behind his house. Most were fitted with exotic hardwoods and etched brass (more like shotgun stocks than axe handles and cross-cut saws), and none were plastic, aluminum, electric, or rechargeable. He still loved to admire them, and when I was a child I, too, marveled at them. "Show what this does," I would command, pointing at a most beautiful or complicated gadget, and he would obligingly demonstrate dado cuts or mortise-and-tenon joinery. Among his tools my father's grandfather also kept several tortoiseshell-encased fountain pens. I regret now that I never asked how they were used, smugly thinking I knew their purpose.

Most professions involve writing, and some composition course designs incorporate training for specific professional applications. Writing-across-the-curriculum approaches usually begin with the assumption that good writing follows similar principles in any profession. The pedagogical supposition is that if people in all professions practiced the clear, colorful rhetorical style prevalent in the humanities, the whole world of discourse would be much improved.

Essay assignments in writing-across-the-curriculum classes usually involve student investigations of current issues in their major fields of study or in proposed career areas. These might include papers exploring factors governing the students' career choices, explaining complicated work-related processes to a general audience, interviewing professionals currently engaged in their chosen careers, and researching technical or controversial topics, practices, or legislation relevant to their job interests. Students who begin college with lofty goals and enthusiasm for their chosen field of study (as many do) are uniquely challenged by this approach. Writing across the curriculum seems particularly relevant to students' career education, and they frequently give composition class the level of effort and attention usually reserved for major-field coursework. (Any really engaging writing class can elicit such participation.) Students without definite career goals can also benefit from a writing-across-the-curriculum approach; you can encourage them to take stock of their interests and aptitudes in early assignments and to explore different career options in depth as part of each of the expository essay projects.

As you can see, a sequence of writing-across-the-curriculum topics readily adapts to process and modes approaches as well. Course design can move from introspective to expository writing and, if students are encouraged to write for a general audience (which is probably best suited to their level of experience), classroom discussion of revisions remains feasible. Writing for a general audience is also a great method of clarifying technical information for oneself (as you will see when you begin explaining the more nebulous aspects of composition style and strategy to student writers). When students' essay topics are customized around their individual areas of expertise, class meetings can still encompass common elements of basic rhetoric, grammar, and punctuation issues.

Writing in the Disciplines

Writing in the disciplines is another career-oriented approach to writing-class content. Given that various professions evolve their own standards and forms for writing, the writing-in-the-disciplines approach allows students to develop universal desirable writing traits (e.g., clarity and standard grammar and punctuation) while learning to conform to specific professional genres (e.g., scientific research reports, medical charting, architectural proposals, or legal briefs).

Although any writing instructor can offer helpful advice in most rhetorical situations, teaching students to write in different academic specialty areas is especially demanding. Beginning students can research the kinds of writing practiced in their proposed academic fields, but their instructor also should be familiar with those models. Ideally, composition instructors team-teach with faculty from other academic departments to facilitate writing-in-the-disciplines instruction. Writing programs in other disciplines are the ultimate in career-relevant writing instruction, but they may be beyond the purview of the average freshman writing course.

Combined Courses

More modest cross-disciplinary writing courses can be arranged with the cooperation of another academic department and the university's scheduling system. Combined courses that simultaneously involve the same group of students in composition and another freshman general education requirement course (i.e., Western civilization, philosophy, biology, or mathematics) can be arranged so that students practice their writing skills while recording and researching content material from the other class. For example, a class of students taking both biology and composition would be asked to write about scientific issues discussed in the biology class. Course combining usually necessitates that the composition instructor sit in on the students' other common class.

Generally, cross-disciplinary approaches to teaching writing are ambitious undertakings. Composition teachers must familiarize themselves with writing styles in other disciplines—either through research or by initiating team-teaching situations. If you are going to help students with work in other academic areas, it is a good idea to become educated about the major issues in their fields. You may also sometimes need to attend classes or be available to consult with students and faculty in other departments. Additionally, composition class time will occasionally be sacrificed to clarifying content issues in the other disciplines involved or to continuing discussions initiated in other classes. Cross-disciplinary writing instruction does provide a ready source of content in an otherwise "contentless" course, and it can assure you and your students that their writing is indeed relevant to their continued work, both in college and in their careers. College students tend to be career-minded, so it is probably a good idea to suggest (even informally) that students write about vocational issues sometime during the term.

Individual Assignments

Everybody has good ideas about the things he or she works at or just dreams of accomplishing one day, and you probably have a lot of good ideas about how to organize and teach a course in written communication. Maybe you have plotted out some assignments or even a complete course in composition that is all your own. If your ideas are consistent with the objectives and sequence of assignments in the department's required course, and if they are within the abilities of your students, they are worth trying out. Design a course you are eager to teach. Writing teachers quickly discover that variety, flexibility, and enthusiasm for the work make classes more engaging and tend to produce better student writing. Excitement is contagious, and if you and your students devote creative energy to class projects, the results will be satisfying.

Remember that all good assignments begin with concrete learning objectives. For example, as an exercise to prepare the class to think critically and organize more complex arguments in a research paper, you might ask your students to compose a letter to the editor of the university newspaper concerning a campuswide controversy. The objectives of the lesson might be to practice inventing and arranging arguments and to gain experience with persuasive writing. But be careful that the class maintains its focus. It could be interesting to learn where your students stand on a moral or ethical issue, and they may be eager to record their opinions on the matter. It even would be exciting to have one or some of their letters published in the paper, but the pragmatic purpose of the exercise is what makes it a good assignment. Composition classes are engaged not simply in text production and evaluation but in the orchestrated development of rhetorical competency.

As you incorporate original lessons into the overall plan for your course, make certain they fit in logically with the sequence of the class. Coursework should move from the more personal forms and purposes of writing (invention, narration, imagination) to more sophisticated constructs of audience and aim (exposition, argumentation, research). For instance, if you want to require students to compose their own family memoir, that should occur early in the course, when students are inventing topics and text from memory. But if you are giving them the assignment of interviewing family members and constructing a history based on their own and others' recollections, the inclusion of secondary material will create a far more complex rhetorical construct, one that would be feasible only after instruction in expository (and perhaps research) writing.

Fortuitous events revised my composition class syllabus one autumn when a National Public Radio correspondent moved into the apartment next door during the week I was preparing fall semester courses. One day when her car broke down I drove her to work and came home inspired to incorporate an interview paper into my course syllabus. Her news-reporting assignment had been to gather information about farm auctions resulting from government foreclosures on agribusiness loans. We followed one unpaved country lane after another, chasing down leads she had assembled by telephone the day before. Everywhere we went generations of farm families and neighbors were anxious to tell their stories—some angry, others sad. One big-shouldered man shook with sobs, apologizing to his grandfather who had been deeded the farm by land grant. The tape recorder ran all the while. There was idle machinery, unwary cattle, rich coffee, and sugary pies to comment upon, too. By early afternoon my interesting new neighbor had sympathetically collected over two hours of audiotapes. We rushed back to the studio while she made notes in a ragged spiral-bound book. That evening, her seven-minute news segment was filled with pathos, indignation, and information. It succinctly captured our morning's adventure, as well as the profundity of the national situation. Condensed from our shared experience, my neighbor's resulting news story was a fascinating writing exercise. The textbooks I was then using made no mention of interview writing, but with prose models clipped from magazines and my new neighbor's promise to consult with the class, I forged ahead, not exactly sure what quality of student essay I could expect.

My objective in the assignment was clear: to practice summarizing original research as preparation for incorporating library materials into the research paper. Still, I was uneasy about requiring the interview because I wondered if students would choose to incur the travel and long-distance telephone costs that in many cases would be needed to indulge my experiment. My neighbor, who interviewed both famous and obscure subjects every week, advised the student writers to try for their first choices but to seek content over celebrity. Empowered, the students enthusiastically sought fascinating personalities and topics, envisioning their papers as magazine cover stories or radio broadcasts. The result was fantastic.

Students interviewed luminaries in world and regional sports and in national and local politics, along with an array of various recognized experts and some subjects of human-interest stories. More impressive, however, was the overall quality of their papers. In their enthusiasm for their subject matter, the students had also devoted extraordinary attention to the organization and presentation of their material. The interview paper has remained, more or less, a staple on my composition syllabus.

MAKING DECISIONS

As you determine the course and contents of your class syllabus, recognize that you probably will want to amend it every term you teach. Writing teachers are always scouting out new assignments to add variety and breadth to their courses. In that sense, every course plan is a "tentative" syllabus; its assignments and even the pedagogical theory behind it are on trial use, subject to revision or replacement. Incidentally, it is useful to label any syllabus you distribute to students "Tentative," thereby granting yourself leeway to make alterations throughout the term as new ideas occur to you—or as lessons take more or less time than you projected and you fall behind or move ahead of schedule.

Before you finalize, duplicate, or distribute your course plan, make sure it is consistent with the master syllabus and catalog descriptions of the class published by the university. The department or program sponsoring the class you teach will have objectives and guidelines that ensure consistency among different sections of the class. Typically, those will include the number and range of essays required of students, the learning objectives specified for the course, and any general policies regarding attendance, plagiarism, grievance procedures, and other such matters. The department may also keep examples of other instructors' syllabi on file; request copies of those or ask individual teachers for copies from their files. Others' course plans are invaluable resources in determining your own syllabus, and most fellow teachers will not mind if you imitate their schemes—or ask for assistance. If you are assigned a teaching adviser, mentor, faculty friend, or boss, show that person the syllabus you propose using in your course. Someone familiar with the specific university, program, course, and students you will be working with should check your outline for accuracy and for the feasibility of its implementation. One of the rewards of teaching is exchanging ideas with peers, so seek friendly counsel as soon as you have some plans on paper.

CHAPTER 2

Classroom Instruction

LECTURE

Hackneyed images of grave professors blandly expounding on esoteric trivia may dominate the public perception of university teaching, but, as you know from your own experience, it is hard to find a remote, dispassionate Kingsfield (from *The Paper Chase*) on our campuses today. A wider variety of students are admitted to colleges each year, and faculty are expected to be personable teachers as well as astute researchers. As an instructor of English composition, you may have competing obligations (such as graduate study, family commitments, deputy administrative assignments, organizational commitments, and avoiding fallout from university politics), but your first duty to your students is to come prepared to lead each day's lesson. As the instructor assigned to a section of composition class, you are the writing teacher on whom those students depend.

The organization of a composition class meeting is quite different from that of a typical college lecture. Concerned with the acquisition, practice, and development of skills rather than with the strict dissemination of information, writing teachers do not frequently lecture, in the usual sense. However, at times you will dominate the ongoing conversation in your classroom, as when you are issuing new assignments, detailing organizational options for essays, simplifying a difficult grammatical concept, or presenting a research-documentation system. Even so, you will probably find that fewer than one-third of your lessons could be described as lectures.

When you do address the class as a whole, presenting your (or your textbooks') point of view entirely, you should try to keep the students involved. Don't let lecturing duties change the essential nature of your course or the dialogue you have established with your students on their papers and during class discussions. Although it may be comforting at first to write out your lectures, try to address the class from notes that leave you the flexibility to change course in response to a student question and to divide time between looking at your notes and making eye contact with the class. I find that a sparse word outline works best for lectures because the energy and adrenaline required to "invent" examples and reconstruct content keeps me focused on the subject, not bored with its mere delivery. As a result, the lecture is less boring to the students, too.

Ask your students to take notes. You may find that they do not expect to take down what is said in a writing class. The course content may seem too abstract or commonsensical to necessitate note taking, but distilling lecture information into an outline is an important cognitive process that helps students digest and remember what has been said—even if they never review those notes again. Help your students learn to take notes in a "contentless" course. You might photocopy and distribute to the class an outline of your first lecture, demonstrating the kinds of points they should record in their own notes. (Circulating outlines of all your lectures, however, encourages student apathy, since they might reason that key points are included on the outline and that they can just review those later instead of attending to your explanations and elaborations.) Using the chalkboard frequently during lectures usually ensures that students will take down whatever you write in front of them, so it is a good idea to put key words and concepts on the board while you address the class.

Ask questions during the lecture, especially open-ended questions without specific right or wrong answers. Pull your students in by drawing your examples from their ideas. For instance, if you are lecturing on the concept of *thesis*, ask students about the papers on which they are working. What are their topics? Who are their audiences? Why are they telling this information to that audience? Elicit theses (and other relevant details) from your students instead of lecturing from abstract, hypothetical examples.

Encourage students to ask questions during your lecture. Remind them to seek clarification immediately whenever they are confused. When one student has a question and is willing to risk asking it in front of others, at least three more students usually are similarly confused and too shy or apathetic to interrupt a lecture. As you talk to your classes, you will probably develop a style in which you continuously seek feedback—perhaps by making queries, such as, "Is this clear?" or "Are we all on the same page with this?" You could also ask students to summarize the principles you have just outlined, or to apply them to their own work.

Develop an interactive style. Some classrooms are furnished with a lectern or even a podium for lecturing, and at first you may find that helpful for holding your notes, establishing your authority, or even giving you a sense of security. Most writing teachers I know eventually eschew such cumbersome barriers and simply stand before their students with notes in hand, sit atop the instructor's desk, or occupy the same sort of seating issued to the students. As you become more secure in your role as teacher (and more familiar with the material you present), you will find that you can move freely around the room while you lecture. Doing so will enable you to interact easily with individual students as well as the whole group while you present material.

Lecturing, holding the attention of a class for fifty minutes or more on a topic most did not choose to study, is a performance art. All of us have studied under professors whose lectures were lively and entertaining or radically unpredictable yet informative. Perhaps some of us go into teaching because we didn't have Wayne Newton's agent to book us at Tahoe, or we look forward to having an audience readily disposed to laugh at our jokes. Students usually appreciate humor in the classroom—as long as it's not at their expense, the course objectives remain clear, and the content of the lessons is primarily relevant to the purpose of the instruction. In general, students have high expectations for the content of their college courses. Naturally, not everyone who chooses to teach is an aspiring ringmaster, and that certainly is not a requirement in the profession. Whether your course offers entertainment or not, the most important qualities to communicate during lectures and class discussions are sincerity and a willingness to help students improve their writing. An evident investment in your students and your subject matter will win student loyalty and respect, which contribute greatly to the popularity of a course or an instructor.

SMALL GROUPS

The standard-issue classroom is equipped with rows of tables or individual student desks that line up course participants like eggs in a carton—evenly spaced and with their yolks perfectly suspended at center to avoid shake-ups or collisions. You will probably want to tamper with that almost immediately. The typical writing class involves a variety of activities that break away from the usual lecture format. If it is possible to rearrange your classroom furniture, you may want to place the chairs or desks in a circle, so that no one occupies the "back row" during class discussions. Sometimes, for part or all of the class period, you may want to shuffle the class meeting further by allowing students to confer or study among themselves in small groups.

Small groups work well for collaborative projects, such as outlining a prose model or brainstorming details, points of comparison, arguments, and so on. Small-group discussions of course material and guided revisions can help students focus their work. (See Peer Editing in Chapter 7.) Although writing is a highly individualized and sometimes lonely activity, its aims are almost always public and social. Awareness of audience (besides the teacher) gives students a reason to write. Working together and writing for an audience of one another develops students' understanding of the communication process. In most classes, students become acquainted socially during the few minutes they are assembled before class; small-group interaction in class reinforces that dynamic, making the connection between peer group and writing audience explicit.

If you devise in-class, small-group activities carefully, the noisy rumble that emanates from conferring groups will have a satisfyingly productive sound. Groups work best with three to six members. Larger groups can be the most productive but also run a greater risk of excluding members or degenerating into aimless conversation. Human beings are very social, and we tend to align ourselves with groups of people whom we identify with or find attractive. Observe your students for a week or so. If you do not impose a seating arrangement, they will organize their own groups within a couple of class meetings: the eager, the affected, the disaffected, the fashion-conscious, the athletic, the nontraditional, the hometown best friends, the acquaintances from other classes, and so on. This is only natural human behavior, but it is not always conducive to productive learning groups. After a week or two, make small-group assignments—you probably will want to change them as the term progresses and each group eventually becomes too predictable. As you orchestrate small-group make-up, your students may grumble a bit, and you may feel like an Orwellian social engineer. Just remember that this is an effort to help them learn, not a match-making exercise; breaking up classroom cliques will facilitate sincere effort and the inclusion of all participants in the groups' deliberations.

Students usually recognize that when small-group work is assigned during class time, they have an obligation to stay on task. Lack of direction is the main reason small groups waste time or degenerate into gossip sessions. When instructors give class time over to small-group work, they are not handing over to students the responsibility for leading the class. Small-group work assignments should be specific and clear. Before breaking your class into groups, spend time with the whole class going over what you expect from them. For example, if students are to read and outline one another's drafts, specify that each student should read his or her entire draft to the group while each member composes an outline of that draft; when those outlines are finished (specify whether individually or collaboratively), the next student may begin reading. Groups whose members are uncertain about their task will lose time debating procedures.

Written agendas help ensure group productivity. Put group work assignments in writing. For example, you might outline the assigned activity or provide a list of questions that each individual or the entire group is expected to answer during the exercise. Asking group members to turn in written work at the end of their meeting helps students to focus on their task. Output—be it a paragraph-long evaluation of group performance, individualized written work, a group-generated outline of activities—will remind students of the purpose of their meeting.

What will you do while your students confer in their small groups? The temptation exists to get a cup of coffee and a copy of the student newspaper and to delve into an editorial about the latest campus controversy. But your actions during small-group work in class will greatly determine your students' attitudes toward the assignment. Used to taking their cues from you on all of their composition assignments, they will continue to use your behavior as a gauge for the intensity of their own concentration and contributions. Pull up a chair and join the group that you suspect is most in need of your added direction. Set the group in motion by appointing a group recorder, soliciting a volunteer to read his or her paper first, or asking whether group members understand the group's task and purpose. Look around at other groups and make sure they are off to a similarly energetic start. Be prepared to leave your group at any time if another meeting of students raises a question or seems to be stalled. Move from group to group, trying to sit in on each gathering long enough to influence its productivity. Ask questions that elicit student input, but don't do the group's work. Watch yourself; don't contribute too much when you sit in on student groups. Give up enough control so that students express their ideas and opinions freely within their group.

At the end of the class meeting, it is a good idea to call all the students back together and comment on the group work that has just concluded. What did they accomplish? How does that tie in with the next assignment? Collect any materials due from groups or individual members. Issue reminders about upcoming assignments, special meetings, or due dates. Small-group exercises work best when they are presented as an activity framed by an ongoing class meeting rather than as an interruption or a recess from regular instruction.

INDIVIDUAL REPORTS

Composition class time is usually consumed by talking about writing issues and practicing incremental writing tasks, but the bulk of serious invention, research, and composition takes place outside the confines of the classroom, on the students' own time and in their own favorite studying places. Individual student reports presented in class meetings can provide a good forum for describing work in progress and for receiving audience response. They are especially productive when students are in the mid-planning stage on a large writing project, such as an interview, argument, or research paper. Class meetings can give them immediate feedback on the direction (scope, thesis, evidence, or organization) of their proposed, outlined or drafted essays. Occasionally, too, you will believe you have said all you can about a particular assignment, but the students will still require time to prepare their essays; individual reports keep class meetings focused on the ongoing project until it is due.

Essentially, a workshop atmosphere prevails during class time when individual reports are presented about an essay in progress. Reports might range from a simple description of the types of sources and kinds of information a student's research has revealed, to a polished speech, carefully crafted to win the audience over to the writer's point of view on a controversial subject. Reading drafts of a complete manuscript to the entire class usually consumes too much time and taxes the other students' attention span too severely to be productive. A better use of class time might be to have students report on the general outline of their drafts, explaining why they chose to include various points of information or how they hope to persuade readers with argumentative strategies. Early research on the composing process suggests that talking through a proposed essay helps students invent ideas and plan strategies, and presenting work in rough form to an audience helps shape writers' awareness of readers as they marshal their thoughts into final form.

Individual reports seem to work best in composition class if they are approached as a somewhat larger version of small-group work—that is, if they are informal and are presented in a context that is positive and supportive. Ten to twenty minutes per report, including group discussion time, is usually a productive length. Large-group interaction tends to require an experienced facilitator, which will be your role as you elicit audience responses to the individual reports. Following a student's report, direct your questions to the other students to elicit audience response: What is the thesis of the proposed paper? What is most striking about the information presented? Could the author say more about some aspect of the topic? Avoid answering your own questions or responding directly to the student who gave the report. Otherwise you will disenfranchise the rest of the class, and you might as well be conducting the conversation as a private conference. As much as possible, use individual reports to engage students in advising each other during early stages of the writing process.

CONFERENCES

If you just announce convenient office hours and keep them assiduously, waiting with a ready smile on your face and your mind open to help students write for any of their classes, you will probably be lonelier than a Maytag repairperson. A few students who have learned to seek out their teachers' guidance will initiate office appointments with you, but few others will drop by for conferences unless your office is centrally and prominently located (such as beside the espresso machine at a popular campus hangout).

When student-initiated conferences do take place, they take on a variety of forms. Students who want to improve their grades sometimes will schedule an appointment, but if their problem is failed work, the best you can offer them is a postmortem investigation, which will be no consolation at all. If this happens, try shifting the focus of the meeting to the next assignment, and discuss ways the student could make a promising start on that. You might also schedule a later meeting with disappointed writers, to take place when their next essay is in progress. Generally, though, it's a better idea to meet with students before grave confrontations are necessary.

Another form of conference is the spontaneous miniconference. The first time you dismiss your class and find yourself amid a throng of eager faces waiting to tell you about past writing accomplishments and defeats or continuing goals and problems, you will be overwhelmed by student mini-conferences. Don't treat these serendipitous after-class meetings lightly; advice is often best heeded when it is most needed. Students who approach you with questions after class usually are searching for a solution to a specific problem. Your support and sound advice at that time not only will influence their current work directly but may also prompt them to seek your counsel more frequently. Brief discussions and chance meetings can be meaningful opportunities for instruction, and some of your best work may take place in these impromptu teaching situations. If your schedule can possibly accommodate it, take time to discuss work with students who wait for you after class, match pace with you on the sidewalk, approach you in the library, or frequent the same neighborhood record store when you do.

The spontaneous conference answers specific questions or solves problems for outgoing students with good timing, but you cannot rely on such informal meetings to keep you in touch with the writing process of the entire class. More structured formal conferences offer the best opportunities for individualized writing instruction. Two required individual conferences per student each term provides a good amount of one-on-one contact. If your teaching load and other responsibilities make more than one required meeting with each student too taxing, you might find out whether your department allows instructors to cancel regular class meetings and hold conferences instead. Used sparingly, such substitutions of instructional mode are very effective. When students are absorbed in their own writing, ten or fifteen minutes of individual conference time can be far more effective in their learning than would be an hour of general in-class instruction.

Formal conferences need not be very long. Ten minutes will often allow you time to read through a short student essay draft, engage in dialogue, and draw up an agenda for continued progress or revision. To schedule such conferences, I photocopy the appropriate pages of my daily planner/schedule, having first blocked out the times I will not be available. I then circulate the pages in class, instructing students to choose an available time and pencil themselves in for meetings in my office. I post those pages on my office door, so that students who forget their appointments can easily look them up and those who need to reschedule can fill in another time or trade with a classmate. When conferences are densely scheduled, you will have to caution students against tardiness and keep yourself on time as well. Otherwise you will have a backlog of disgruntled students in the hallway.

I believe conferences are the most effective format for writing instruction, but each conference requires as much planning and finesse as a regular class meeting. As a young teacher, I struggled against my own triage mentality on conference days, often feeling like an emergency room physician in a disaster area as I strove to "treat 'em and street 'em." Each student represented a different problem, another immediate symptom to alleviate, as I sat at my desk, sleeves rolled up, giving orders. Eventually I realized (and students were instrumental in teaching me this) that such a heedlessly authoritarian approach was counterproductive to the purpose of conferencing. Marking papers is a monologue, but the writing conference should be a dialogue between teacher and student in which the writers of papers are allowed to own their own work. Don't be quick to appropriate the students' texts. Listen as much as you talk, and take advantage of the opportunity to ask as well as tell in conferences.

Your instruction will be most effective if you require students to bring a manuscript in progress to their conferences; that may be prewriting on two or three proposed topics, an outline, a few paragraphs, or an entire rough draft. Good ideas alone do not demonstrate sufficient thought and effort toward the assignment and do not provide a body of work to discuss; insist on written work as the subject of each writing conference.

It helps to begin each conference with some typical but brief exchange of pleasantries. If you have trouble matching names with faces in class, conference interaction may help you learn who your students are. Ask for the text your student has brought for discussion. When I read over text in a conference, I usually read aloud to its author. I explain first that I know how nerve wracking it can be to watch as someone silently reads my work, and that reading aloud is the best way I can devise to give writers an idea of how their work sounds in the voice and thoughts of a reader. I do not mark up students' papers as I read them in conference. Marking interrupts the flow of the text and can cause the conference to degenerate into a typical grading exercise. I do ask the student questions about the paper: its details, intended thesis, changes since earlier drafts. What does the writer like best about the work? What questions does he or she have?

The purpose of the writing conference is not to fix text on the spot, but to provide students with the direction and motivation to continue work on their assignments. As you offer your evaluation and your recommendations for the next step in the writing process, be encouraging. There are some good things you can say about every work, and it is those—not the problems to be solved—that will inspire students to sit down and rework the assignment. If the text you examine in conference has a lot of problems, use this meeting to address only those that are the most pressing. For instance, if a paper's topic is poorly focused or inadequately limited and the text also contains several egregious grammar errors, state your concerns about only the topic and recommend ways to improve that area. Then schedule a later conference. If the grammar problems persist in the next draft (and they usually do), you can discuss those during your next meeting.

As you become more at ease with one-on-one instruction, you will discover that it improves regular class meetings as well. Many students who have engaged in conference dialogue with you will become much more glib in class, enthusiastically volunteering their work or their opinion for class discussion. If conference meetings are a helpful, positive experience, students not only will enjoy class time more but also may initiate conferences themselves. When group and individual meetings begin to reinforce one another, you are teaching in an optimal learning environment.

WORD PROCESSING

Undoubtedly, late twentieth-century availability and advancement in computer technology has changed the writing process, and several other everyday tasks, forever. As computers and terminals are added to classrooms, residence halls, libraries, and bookbags all over campus, the changes wrought by hardware, software, and network servers exponentially expand the concept of literacy. The dim lights burning late at night often signify students hunched over computer screens, deep into coursework, or into simulation or elaborate fantasy games; many are engaged on the networks in the most eclectic conversation in town or around the globe. One student recently confessed his first-date anxiety to me. It was the eve of his initial face-to-face meeting with a woman with whom he had corresponded on a campus computer network for more than a year. I advised him to relax; he and his electronic penpal obviously had more in common than did the first dates of my generation. "But," he sputtered with the frustration common to all who try to codify culture, "my writing is a more interesting person than I am!" His fear, perhaps, reveals the magic of composing on the computer; it is an anonymous tool that allows us to invent, reinvent, and improve on our work (and therefore ourselves) without a hint of betrayal of anything that has come before.

The extent to which you use computers in your composition classroom will in part depend on the availability of hardware and how it is configured (in a network or as a terminal connected to a mainframe computer). Some software has been developed specifically for use in writing classrooms. Heuristic programs, for instance, help students with prewriting by posing questions based on Aristotle's *topoi*, discourse modes, or communication-triangle aims. Generally, if you can schedule your class to meet periodically in a computer lab with any word processing software and enough workstations for your students, you can make productive use of computer technology in your course.

Word processing is a useful tool for requiring students to draft essays during class time, especially near the beginning of the term. In such sessions, you will be available to answer questions as they arise, and those students who otherwise might not expend such focused effort on the assignment will be supervised in a sustained period of concentration and preliminary writing.

Word processing also offers other advantages for in-class writing assignments. As you probably know from your own experience, writing on the computer is usually a much more fluid process than is creating hard copy with a pen or a typewriter. The ability to pursue an idea as it occurs and, if necessary, to delete it easily at some later time decreases frustration, especially in high-pressure writing situations like drafting papers in class. Many students who are required to write in class with a pen and paper waste a great deal of time copying and recopying their work as they change their minds and decide to add or delete a sentence or two. Computer composition virtually eliminates this compulsion because the word processing program automatically reformats altered pages. For those who are afraid to change their drafts—worrying that the first, no matter how flawed, may be their best work—the computer provides simple methods for saving multiple variations of a single draft.

Using word processing for in-class writing makes it possible to generate multiple copies of every student's work quickly and easily. If printers are available in the lab where you meet, you can ask students to copy their drafts for you to review as well as print their own copies so that they can continue their writing as homework. Students can also copy their work on diskettes, for later editing; writers without private access to compatible computers can return to the lab to complete their work. You also have the option of collecting diskette copies of student work, reading them on the computer, making changes and comments on the text, and then saving your version under a new file name. When you return students' diskettes, they will then contain both your marked version of the text and the original draft intact.

Word processing programs are paradoxically more complex and simpler to use with every version on the market. If you require all students to use the same program in class (such as Word or WordPerfect), you will have to devote one or two class periods to instruction in the fundamentals of the program. Students will need this time to practice configuring pages, selecting fonts, cutting and pasting documents, saving and printing text, and running the spell checker or other ancillary programs.

Even with typing and handwriting there exists a disparity of skills between students, but on the computer those seem to be magnified. Some will become virtual word processing experts within a week, and others will never remember how to boot the machine and start the program. The computer in the writing classroom also adds a new dimension to late work. When students must compete for the use of terminals in computer laboratories, there will always be problems with availability. Some students will undoubtedly be unable to hand in their papers on time because the lab was shut down for repairs or because no terminals were available the night before the essay was due. Additionally, if the systems linking terminals with printers are complex, some students will invariably believe they have sent their work out to Mars for printing, from where even the best crackerjack computer lab supervisor is unable to call it back. Of course, pens and pencils fail, too. In sum, the benefits of reinforcing students' writing skills through their computer aptitudes outweigh the liabilities.

If you think of computers as creative tools, like cameras or recording studios, you will come up with more uses for word processors in the composition class than their obvious role as electronic typewriters. An enjoyable and productive word processing exercise developed by two of my colleagues is an anonymous draft-editing procedure. Each student brings to class a complete draft of the current essay assignment on diskette and loads it into a terminal, renaming it to create a second file so that the original remains unchanged on the disk. When everyone's essay is loaded, the instructor calls for students to trade terminals. Each student then becomes an "editor" of the manuscript on the screen before him or her. The editors are asked to treat the text as if it were their own, reviewing and revising it for publication. Every fifteen or twenty minutes, all editors are asked to change terminals again. At the end of the exercise, students return to their original workstations and save the edited version of the essay for later review and comparison with the original intact draft.

COMPUTER CONFERENCING

Computer programs also can be used to facilitate group discussions. Various software and networking capabilities permit users to converse with participants in the same classroom, around campus, or around the world. Computer conferences can examine the same topics as those explored in classroom discussions. Students can respond to questions or prompts posted by their instructors, or they can enter drafts or parts of essays into the computer and then respond to one another's papers or comments concerning the essays.

Real-time conferencing software (including Interchange, Aspects, and Real-Time Writing) allows students to converse among themselves, with their messages appearing on networked computer screens immediately as they release them for publication. Such programs are easy to use and require only a few minutes' orientation. Students simply type out statements and enter them; the software distributes the messages to all participating classmates. Everyone can "talk" simultaneously, and the rapidity with which real-time conferencing serves messages across the network causes the electronic interaction to closely resemble a fast-paced, face-to-face debate. At the end of the computer-aided discussion, the entire conversation can be electronically sorted (by topic or speaker) and printed for classroom discourse analysis or continuation of the discussion.

If your school does not own any real-time software, you can emulate it using a campus electronic mail system. This is slightly cumbersome and slower than the software intended for classroom discussion, but its effect is the same. Ask a computing specialist to help you compose a mail distribution list of the members of your class and to help you simplify mail commands and create an orientation lesson for students. You can post assignments and mail them to students via the distribution. Students can send drafts of their papers or compose discussion messages at terminals in the classroom and mass-mail them to one another. Because mail discussions do not operate within the context of a software shell, you will not be able to manipulate the data and may have trouble printing a copy of the discourse.

Larger, worldwide networks provide a forum for discussions on virtually any topic. You might spend a class meeting helping students log onto an international network or bulletin board (through Internet, Bitnet, or Usernet) and encouraging them to enter into discussion far outside the classroom. The abstract concept of audience becomes startlingly real to students when their ideas generate a pointed response from a distant network user. Students quickly learn that composition class lessons are relevant to all writing; the comments entered into a network bulletin board become part of the fabric of an elaborate discourse—in which all writers, students included, may be lauded or held accountable for their contributions. Networks automatically bring interaction with the "real world" into the writing classroom. Students may want to learn to download news, essays, or information from international networks to use in their research papers.

Discussion conducted over electronic media differs markedly from normal classroom conversation. The anonymity of the situation reduces students' inhibitions about talking in class. In fact, the faceless computer screen seems to distance students' thoughts from their identities. Electronic-conversation participants compose their "speech" on their private screens before releasing it to the public, so they have the opportunity to craft their contributions exactly, without fear of misspeaking or interruption. They also have the writer's option of determining the "voice" they wish to present to the audience. Computer discussions are an amalgam of conversation and publication situations. They tend to elicit casual comments as well as rhetorically orchestrated discursive statements. Once sent, an electronic message becomes text in someone else's database—to be read, stored, printed, or altered. The conversation is published. Computer conferencing comes close to bridging the gap between speaking and writing. In the postfax, postmodem electronic age of our students' lifetimes, distinctions between speaking and writing or between copying and publishing may dissolve. We cannot teach our students to use the inventions of their futures; we can only prepare them to adapt.

CHAPTER 3

Assignments

WRITING ASSIGNMENTS

The first time I lectured in front of a writing class, I caught myself rambling nearly incoherently about attitudes toward writing. To extricate myself from my endless monologue without seeming to falter, I suggested that students "jot down their attitudes toward writing" for our next meeting. The next day I casually asked the twenty-four assembled students if anyone had remembered to attempt my little assignment. To my astonishment, two dozen notebooks snapped open to reveal four dozen pages of neatly prepared text. The awesome power of the writing assignment loomed between the lines of meticulously recopied homework. I realized that, as teachers, we must heed the old Chinese proverb and be careful about what we wish. When we issue assignments, most of our students knock themselves out by assiduously trying to complete them. We therefore have a duty to think through our assignments carefully, to be as specific as possible about our expectations, and to be reasonable about our requirements.

There are many assignments that help students develop writing skills without imposing the pressure inherent in formal essay requirements. Of course, essays play an important role in composition class, but a course developed around several different levels of writing assignments will be more interesting and helpful to students. Simple writing exercises that foster a high degree of success will also encourage students to expend more effort and achieve better style in their formal essays.

Diagnostic Essays

Most writing classes begin with the assignment of a diagnostic essay. This clinical-sounding name derives from the fact that the resulting writing sample helps teachers "diagnose" students' writing abilities and problems.

It also introduces students to college writing assignments, revision methods, and grading standards.

Assign the diagnostic essay as early as possible, usually within the first week of class. Provide a prompt that is general and requires no more than common knowledge about a topic. The less directive your assignment is, the more easily you will discover what your students have learned about inventing and organizing an essay. I have simply asked students to respond to the question, "In general, is life fair or unfair?" This tactic quickly reveals whether students have learned to focus or customize a topic, whether they are adept in stating a thesis, and how well they use examples.

You can use the diagnostic essay solely for your own information in deciding the kinds of specific lessons that will benefit most of your students. But if you are planning to emphasize the writing process in your class, you may want to closely guide students' revisions of their diagnostic essays to demonstrate the level of rewriting you will require in your course.

Just as diagnostic essays suggest what instructors can expect from students during the term, they also show students how the instructor will evaluate and grade their work. I mark the final version of diagnostic essays as rigorously as I do any other paper in the course, applauding or challenging the thesis, pointing out grammatical and rhetorical errors, and praising vivid phrases and sophisticated sentence structures. I never consider preliminary work, such as a diagnostic essay, when I determine a student's final course grade, and I make certain that writers are aware that the diagnostic is a practice assignment. Nevertheless, I apply course-grading standards and assign the appropriate grade to each paper, indicating the rank it would merit. The diagnostic essay is often the first college-level evaluation of writing skills that students receive. Although it "doesn't count" in terms of establishing a grade-point average, it will probably be the most important assignment you present and evaluate all term.

Journals

Requiring students to keep journals in a composition class is a good method of reinforcing their daily writing without a corresponding increase in the time you spend reading and marking papers. Although you may ask students to record a page or two in their journals each day, you probably will need to collect and read those notebooks only three or four times per term. (Recognize, naturally, that some students will then write in their journals only three or four times per term, but the most inventive will employ different utensils and handwriting styles to make it seem as if they have been working steadily all along.)

There are several approaches to journal keeping, ranging from Benjamin Franklin's oiled-paper notebook in which he recorded his daily virtues and transgressions, to John Steinbeck's revised *Travels With Charlie*, to Andy Warhol's dictated diaries, and to Le Corbussier's elegant sketchbook/notebooks. If you do not specify the type of journal you expect, many students will gravitate toward personal diaries. However, if students expect that you (and perhaps other class members) will be reading them, their diaries will be uniformly mundane—records of rising times, breakfast menus, course schedules, homework logs, travel itineraries. Public diaries suffer from confusion about audience; although their writers usually try to talk to themselves, they are painfully conscious that others are straining to eavesdrop.

The best journals for composition class are derived from the commonplace book. A commonplace book is a journal in which writers (or painters, or dancers, or mechanical engineers) record interesting ideas for further exploration. For instance, a poet struck by the pathos of an Associated Press (AP) news story from a disaster site might clip it out and preserve it in a commonplace book, along with a few jottings toward a poem on the subject. A student writer might copy down a thought-provoking quotation from a textbook, a fragment of conversation overheard in a dining hall, or the same AP wire story that caught the imagination of the poet. The commonplace book becomes a warehouse of ideas. Students who write out a quick response to the artifacts they collect will find that they have the beginnings of several essays housed in their journals.

There are essentially two ways to use journals or writers' notebooks in composition class: assigning open topics (students decide what they will write about) and assigning directed entries (you determine the topic of the day). If you require students to write in their journals every day, you will probably want to give them some freedom to choose their own topics from time to time. Open topics encourage class members to see themselves as writers and virtually everything around them as potential subject matter. However, students eventually have difficulty sustaining the enthusiasm of self-direction. As initial ideas play themselves out and the demands of more specific assignments take precedence, open-topic journal essays become less inventive and may be abandoned altogether.

Directed entries provide student writers with a framework for invention. Broad topics that allow students to customize the assignment work best: You might, for example, ask your students to go to a local art museum and write about one person or object they view there. Journal assignments can also function as prewriting exercises for essays. For example, when introducing a comparison-and-contrast essay assignment, you might ask students to compose a journal memoir about their favorite place to visit during childhood. The next day, you could direct students to write about the same place on the occasion of their last visit or as they imagine it currently. On subsequent days you might assign similar general topics (a favorite relative and themselves, a famous landmark and a famous person) until they had recorded two or three potential paper ideas. Although you might still urge students to choose their own topics for the final paper, their journal entries would provide practice in inventing and organizing content in a particular mode or strategy.

Journal entries can also help students prepare for class discussion and can reinforce course lessons. For instance, a teacher may ask students to compose a short journal essay on the same topic as a prose model they will be reading later in the week. When the class discusses the prose model, the instructor can ask students to turn to their journal essays and compare their own opinions on the topic with those expressed in the professional article. Similarly, students might be asked to react in their journals to a prose model after it has been discussed in class. Journals can act as an individualized extension of the class meeting—a discussion in which students are encouraged to express their opinions frankly.

Collecting, reading, and marking students' journals can be problematic. If students are expected to write in their notebooks every day, collecting them may disrupt that routine. (Carrying and storing twenty or more large notebooks can also disrupt your routine!) You may want to schedule conferences in which you look over students' journals. Let each student show you the parts he or she likes best, or ask to see a specific assignment. Some teachers frequently remind students that journals are homework, not personal diaries, and that writers should not record secrets in their composition journals. Others permit students to write personal material and cover or staple together pages that are not intended for an audience.

Since the journal is the students' own forum, it may seem invasive or unethical to edit or judge the work in it. Many instructors grade journals solely on their completeness. To encourage students to continue experimenting with different writing styles and voices in the journal, and to protect its status as a high-success activity, grammar and punctuation errors in the journal are usually not penalized and often not marked at all. Because the commonplace book is a collection of ideas, I usually respond to a few of the thoughts recorded there by noting promising paper topics, citing correspondences with prose models, suggesting further reading on a topic, or just heartily seconding or questioning a student's expressed opinion. In general, students follow up more frequently and completely on comments I write on journal entries and other ungraded writings than they do to remarks I make about theme contents. Journal writings become friendly correspondence between us.

Freewriting

One summer in college I signed onto a painting crew that painstakingly applied latex house paint in decorator colors (mostly beige) to clients' residences. I was on trim detail, assigned to a summer of outlining door frames, window sills, shutters, cabinets, doors, and baseboard moldings. In the afternoons, when work ended, I washed the beige emulsion from my hands, arms, and head while I added up my anticipated wages for the day. Then I hurried to catch up with my troupe in summer stock theater, where I could smear paint onto the huge backdrops for the company's sets. It was great fun mixing the dark and bright colors with our bare hands and arms and crawling around on the downed canvases, applying paint with huge brushes, rags, sponges, and other inventive and unlikely utensils—frequently engaged into the middle of the night. It wasn't until later in the year that I realized that my entire summer had been consumed by painting; painting in the theater had been so enjoyable I hadn't connected it with my day job at all.

Writing, as you know, can be a very enjoyable experience, an opportunity to discover and create that is as rewarding as any other artistic endeavor. But to composition students, many of whom have not discovered a connection between formal essay writing and the kinds of writing they enjoy, it is often the grown-up equivalent of being ordered to stay within the lines in a coloring book. Working within an established structure does yield magnificent results (a keenly crafted inductive argument or a moving and rhetorically balanced Petrarchan sonnet), but sometimes, and especially when writers are just starting to work with an idea, the imposition of structure can be limiting. Frequently you will see students with an exciting idea for an essay just sit and stare in frustration at blank paper, unable to convert the idea they have discussed freely into the first draft of class work. Sometimes students will reduce a monumental inquiry to a single sentence or brief paragraph and insist that the topic is exhausted.

A lot of people blame this inability to get words on paper on something called "writer's block," an inability to compose text. However, that's just an excuse; it can't happen. You can prove to your students that writer's block does not exist with a short, simple exercise. In preparation for the demonstration, ask the students to close their eyes for thirty seconds and make their minds blank. Time this precisely—just for the appearance of scientific method. When half a minute has passed, ask if anyone was successful in making his or her mind totally "blank." Of course no one will have been. (Anyone with a completely inactive mind is brain dead and should be excused immediately to go to a hospital emergency room.) There are always thoughts in our heads, even if they seem to be basic or mundane (wanting to eat, wanting to sleep, wanting a pair of shoes like those worn by the person nearby). Writers can always write; they may have trouble writing about topics or structures that have been imposed by assignments or other formal situations, but there is always something we can say, and we can learn to use that to get started on the things we must write.

Freewriting is a heuristic that helps writers move from the topics they want to explore to the ones they must examine. (Heuristics are derived from book two of Aristotle's *Rhetoric*; part of the classical *topoi*, they are literally "places to start," or methods for discovering and developing arguments.) Discussed extensively in Peter Elbow's 1973 book *Writing Without Teachers*, freewriting is a simple but effective technique that can be taught to students on the very first day of class. It replaces the agony of "writer's block" with a few minutes of intense creative activity.

Start in-class freewriting exercises by asking students to produce a pen and two or three sheets of paper, and explain that they will be writing for a specified amount of time. (Elbow suggests freewriting for twenty-minute periods, but I usually start with five- to seven-minute stretches. Most students can sustain that amount of text successfully, and it produces only minimal complaints about "writer's cramp.")

The rules for freewriting are simple: Students must continue to write ceaselessly during the specified block of time. I tell my students to keep their pens constantly moving in a forward direction; they need not even go back to dot *i*'s or cross *t*'s if they can break themselves of that ingrained habit. Freewriters should never read back over their text during the allotted writing time and should not erase or obliterate anything on the page. Also, writers should record every thought that comes to mind; instruct students that no idea is "wrong" or too foolish to include. Finally, writers must commit high energy to the exercise; I like to think of this as condensing all the energy expended in a full afternoon of procrastination into a ten- or twenty-minute flurry. Freewriters waiting for their cue to begin are like track runners, crouched in the blocks, awaiting the starter's pistol. I have even threatened early morning and late afternoon groups (the sleepiest ones) with compulsory calisthenics as a warm-up activity for freewriting; that has a surprisingly bracing effect on the weary.

There are two kinds of freewriting topics: open and directed. In open freewriting, students begin by recording whatever is on their minds, hoping eventually to work their way around to material that will be useful in an upcoming assignment. Open freewriting can be a lot of fun, and it is an all-purpose journal assignment. It does not, however, result in as much useful classroom discussion or prewriting material as does directed freewriting. Directed freewritings can be used to prompt students to think about upcoming theme assignments, react to assigned readings, or respond to issues raised in class or on their papers. Topics for directed freewriting should be sufficiently broad to allow students to customize their writing. For instance, a class preparing to write definition papers might be asked to choose their topics from a list of related terms, such as *justice, freedom, equality, opportunity,* or *democracy*. Since students are to begin writing immediately, without time to brainstorm examples or plan their work, topics should be simple enough to be quickly understood and general enough to

appeal to most writers. You might instruct writers who have trouble starting freewriting exercises to begin by writing, "I can't think of anything. I
can't think of anything." The human mind does not like to be bored. This
repetitious activity usually prompts some more-stimulating thought.

Of course students can freewrite at home, timing themselves with a
wristwatch or even an alarm clock. If you present freewriting as a heuristic
that writers can use to solve invention problems, students will be very
receptive to learning it and will probably try it on their own, too. But
freewriting is also a very useful in-class activity. Initiated at the beginning
of the class period, it helps to settle the students and focus their thinking
on the writing activity in which the class is engaged. Freewriting is also a
quick method of text production, and you can follow it with a class discussion of the writing it generates.

Collecting and reading in-class freewriting reinforces the message that
it is an important activity, but because freewriting is usually presented as
a totally "free"—not screened or edited—composition process, its mechanical correctness is usually not graded. I do not mark spelling, grammar, or
punctuation errors in freewritings. Instead, I make the assumption (which
is usually correct) that the students would correct these problems themselves in a more formal writing situation. Given the writing situation, it is
most fair to limit your comments on freewriting to positive responses to
content or simply to marks indicating that you have read the exercise and
have given the student credit for the assignment.

Freewriting is a high-success activity. Although some students may have
difficulty sustaining continuous writing, almost every student will be able
to generate what constitutes for him or her a good quantity of text in a
short period of time. Many students will discover that their problem with
"writer's block" is the simultaneous fear of preserving an inferior idea or
forgetting it. For instance, a student who has been taught to start a paper
with an attention-getting introduction may be able to think only of a
mundane sentence, such as, "In this paper I am going to talk about three
kinds of recyclable plastic." She knows that is an inadequate start for her
paper, so she is reluctant even to write it down. However, when she tries
to think of a better beginning, that mechanical introduction suggests itself
to her again. In freewriting, she would be encouraged to record that
sentence without judgment. Having preserved it on paper, she then could
move on to more ideas for her essay. Freewriting produces at least a
baseline text, ideas to fall back on if others fail or do not occur. Once
students have *something* on paper, they will more easily relax and take
risks in composing lively discourse.

Freewriting is an amazingly productive prewriting activity. Because the
mind is fairly orderly and one idea prompts the next, recording thoughts
as they occur leads to a better integration of ideas than does a less-focused
activity, such as outlining a proposed paper. The natural flow of the

freewriting text suggests an organizational model for the eventual draft. The intensity of freewriting also prompts writers to invent new ideas as they write. Just as particularly stimulating conversations sometimes lead us to new discoveries about what we think and know, freewriting prompts writers to let the association of thoughts lead them to conclusions they otherwise might not have reached. The production of text also leads to more text. Once writers have something on paper—even relatively disjointed or undeveloped freewriting—they can delete text or add to it, break it into logical divisions and develop those, and research some issues they have raised. A large part of the writing process is the manipulation of text, and freewriting gives students the necessary material to engage in the writing process.

Private Drafts

One day while amusing myself in the university library, I found a book of navigational charts for the Northern Hemisphere and was able to take a fairly exact reading of the longitude and latitude where I sat—in the library with the book in my lap. It was funny, I thought, that this was such a precise measurement of the earth, but the figure in the book represented absolutely nothing of the reality I perceived as I sat at 40°12′ north, 85°23′ west.

An outline is a sort of map of the discourse it describes, and although it may be precise, it also is distant—a minimal abstraction of the paper it measures. Students frequently complain that they cannot write from outlines. Some believe they cannot predict what they will say when they really begin writing in earnest; others find that the abstract outline bears no relation to the text they finally invent. Most rhetoric books and teachers, it seems, are enthusiastic proponents of the outline. We might wonder, of the millions of required outlines turned in with finished college papers, how many were written last?

Private drafts of papers are a compromise between outlines and unplanned writing. They are written for a very specific audience of one: the writer who is discovering what he or she wants to communicate. Parts of the draft may be written in the tone and voice of a public writer, but students are also free to abandon that facade in private drafts, combining elements of outline, or their own internal voice, with their prose. For instance, the private draft of a narrative paper may substitute, instead of a paragraph, the notation, "Tell how it felt to hear the announcement of who had made the team." Or the private draft of a research paper might contain the directive, "Find out the percentage of Japanese cars manufactured in America over the past decade." Students can also list options for the direction of their discourse. An interview writer might note, "Tell about his childhood here"—or—"Tell what made him go into acting in the first place." Most writers find such freeform planning more useful and realistic than typical outlines. Many students have been taught that an outline adheres to a very specific set of formal conventions (indentations, Roman numerals, capital letters, cardinal numbers, lowercase letters). You can explain that such formal outlines are best composed after the text is revised, but prewriting or private drafts can include any form that is helpful in organizing material or jogging the memory of the writer—even pictures, drawings, or private allusions.

Private drafts are particularly useful with expository writing assignments. Students who can outline a topic about which they know little more than its buzzwords are confronted with their dearth of specific information when they try to discuss the subject. The private draft reinforces that cardinal rule about discourse: *Write about what you know*. I assign private drafts as topic proposals for research papers. By collecting and reading the drafts, I am better equipped to guide students in narrowing or changing topics (when necessary) early in the writing process.

Try to confine your comments on private drafts to advice about the content and organization of the proposed paper; mark them as you would an outline. Writers often speak candidly or ask for advice in private drafts, confessing, for instance, "This is really getting boring" or "confusing" or "off my original topic." Such worries indicate an acute awareness of audience and attest to the logical succession from private to public drafts of discourse.

Paragraphs

Especially if your students have difficulty developing entire papers, you may want to spend some time teaching them to write just paragraphs. A textbook-perfect paragraph is an essay in microcosm. Its topic sentence correlates with a paper's thesis, elaboration or development corresponds to an essay's body, and—although a paragraph does not usually have a conclusion—a well-wrought example winds down skillfully or snaps surprisingly to an artful closing. Many of the same rhetorical principles (arrangement, description, definition, persuasion) operate on the level of the paragraph with nearly as much complexity as in longer discourse.

After I work for weeks with a basic composition class on various methods of paragraph development, my students sometimes continue to ask, "How long should paragraphs be?" That is like asking how tall a tree must be or how wide a river, I thought one day, but I answered, "as long as it needs to be to develop its topic sentence." Frustrated that my answer did not satisfy, I impulsively met the familiar question with a more concrete response when a persistent student again demanded to know the acceptable size of a paragraph. "Three to twelve sentences," I quipped. To my dismay, for the remainder of that predictable semester I did not read a paragraph shorter than three or longer than twelve sentences.

Paragraphing problems in student writing reveal themselves quickly in composition class. If you find that your students need help learning to construct paragraphs, limiting a writing assignment to a single paragraph focuses attention on that important element of written discourse. You can invent some short paragraphing assignments, such as asking students to consider their given name: Why was it chosen? What does the name mean? Does it have cultural, literary, or family origins? How well does the bearer like being known by that name?

Many essay prompts can be reduced to paragraph assignments if such concentrated writing will benefit students. For example, working intensely with students to write and revise a descriptive or definition paragraph may meet the educational needs of the class better than extracting whole essays in those modes. And, because papers are constructed one paragraph at a time, the class can momentarily focus on a single paragraph from a larger body of writing—an introductory or concluding paragraph, a descriptive paragraph within a narrative theme, a background paragraph from an interview paper, or a paragraph summarizing a book or an article for a research paper. Specific work on paragraphing will produce noticeable improvement in students' theme organization and development, but you should highlight just one or two paragraphs per essay assignment. If you try as a class to write essays paragraph-by-paragraph, the results will be mechanical and the process will become tedious. There is an element of spontaneity in good paragraphing that gives tone, voice, and pace to written language, and the best way to teach spontaneity is to avoid imposing too much structure.

Essays

During our first year as graduate assistants, my peers and I heard a rumor that at some Ivy League schools composition was taught as "Daily Themes." We were filled with admiration for those students who, according to hearsay, generated a polished college paper in one hour each weekday without benefit of instruction or encouragement. By the end of our first year as teachers, our admiration for those mythical writers turned to sympathy as we discovered the satisfaction earned by instructors and students when a carefully planned assignment gradually produces a student writer's best work.

College writing courses generally depend on the essay as an instructional genre for two reasons: It provides the best proving ground for basic rhetorical principles, and it most closely approximates the writing expected of many students as they continue their college and work careers. Composition class assignments are variously known as essays, themes, or papers. I tell students that I prefer the word *essay* because it derives from the Romance languages' influence on English (since the Norman Conquest) and is closely related to the French word *essai*, which means *to try*. (*Essay*, as a verb, means the same thing in English as well.) The composition essay is an attempt to express oneself completely and competently. When we assign an essay, we are asking students to take a try at the assignment, the prompt, and their topic.

Composition essays are both course examinations and class projects. Students' progress in the course is determined, in large measure, by their performance on themes, and course grades are usually derived from a scheme that weights essay scores heavily over other grades. Essays, therefore, are the most important tests in the course. Like most exams, themes test students' grasp of class lessons; however, themes are not the typical hour-long memory trials of most tests but a gradual (often two- or three-week) process of building evidence of acquired skills. A well-paced, well-organized essay assignment gives students the opportunity to receive a high score on the paper without the last-minute rushing or "cramming" that often accompanies typical college examinations.

A good assignment begins with a written rubric or set of directions. You can write that on the chalkboard, photocopy it as a handout, or—if you are really sure of it (which usually means you have used it at least once already)—include it in your course overview or syllabus. The written assignment should include a brief (one- or two-sentence) definition of the essay expected, such as "You are to write a first-person narrative about a single incident that occurred in your own life and taught you an important lesson." Also list any specific requirements for the paper, such as page length or word count; due dates for outlines, drafts, and revisions; and small-group, peer-editing, or teacher-student conferences. The written assignment becomes an important reference for students, but it is just the tip of the iceberg in terms of the real assignment. The sentence describing the assigned essay in the example refers to many words and concepts that an instructor would have to define in class. To be fully understood by students, the assignment depends on class discussion of "first-person" point of view, the "narrative" mode, focusing a topic on a "single incident," and lessons in establishing and reinforcing a thesis that portrays the "important lesson" learned by the writer. Although you will be able to describe the written assignment in only one paragraph or so, you will find that a week or more of class time will be required to clarify, elaborate on, and experiment with the concepts embodied in that short statement.

Themes and their drafts can be written during class meetings or outside of the classroom. Although students usually express a strong preference for writing on their own, a few in-class writings, especially early in the term, can help shape good writing practice. Daunted by the task, some students will be unwilling to devote sustained effort to theme writing if left to their own devices. In-class writing trains students to give nearly an hour's attention to the project before surrendering. Writing for the duration of one class meeting usually yields enough success that students are motivated to finish their drafts as homework. A lot of students give up on drafting papers on their own because they want an answer to some simple question. Writing in class puts you at their disposal for fifty minutes or so, during which time you can answer such show-stopping questions as "Are we supposed to write on every other line?," "How long is this supposed to be again?" or "Is my thesis wrong?" Additionally, students writing in class model productive behaviors among themselves, such as reexamining the assignment sheet, using an outline, consulting a dictionary, and rereading or proofreading their own text. Because people write best at different rates and in different situations, in-class writing is a better situation for draft production than for essay revision.

Out-of-class writing assignments allow students to fall back on their favorite writing rituals—the things we all do to make ourselves comfortable or to produce an environment conducive to thought. Some people like order or cleanliness; others write best at a desk piled with notes and papers. Because of the tight quarters in residence halls, many students sit or lie on their beds to write. Some prefer absolute silence, while others like to play the stereo or television or to write in a public library or study lounge. Coffee, high-caffeine soda, cookies, pizza, and ice cream are the popular fuels for student writers I know. Most people have a favorite time of day for writing, "lucky" or comfortable clothing, a really slick pen, paper that they like best, and even an attitude they achieve through exercise or meditation. You are probably aware of many of your own writing rituals already, but chances are that most of your students will not have given it much thought. Encourage them to identify their preferences and to distinguish between those that are truly conducive to better writing and those that can be modified and invoked in controlled situations, such as essay examinations or other in-class writing contexts.

Regardless of the type of prompt you assign students to write about (a mode, a thesis, a specific topic), some general rules apply. A good writing assignment is broad enough that students can customize it by choosing their own specific topic, whether that means deciding to compare any two topics in the world or narrowing a rhetorical analysis of Martin Luther King's "I Have a Dream" speech down to his uses of repetition. Students must have some ownership in their topics if they are to expend their best effort.

Teachers also should consider their audience by choosing general prompts that interest students and that are within their area of competence. Our culture tends to idealize college students as being politically aware and active, but the truth is that they are as diverse as the rest of the population. Asking students to write about a specific legal or political issue disenfranchises many enthusiastic writers. You can avoid this problem by framing your assignments so that students can incorporate their own interests into their work.

Good writing assignments should be sequential. Overall, assignments should be arranged from the least to the most rhetorically complex, but each new assignment should build on the skills your students practiced in their previous paper. For instance, narration uses chronological organization, and process analysis depends on it for clarity and successful emulation of the process described. By emphasizing the connections between assignments, you can build students' confidence in their developing abilities and indicate what you expect them to achieve in the new assignment.

Five-paragraph Themes

Regardless of the variety of assignments you issue, you will discover that many of your students have learned to write by formula, adapting every topic to a redundant five-paragraph organizational structure. The outline is simple: An introduction pointedly states the thesis and names the essay's following three main points. Each of these three points is developed in its own paragraph, and a concluding paragraph summarizes the main points and reiterates the thesis. Problems with this widely taught structure include its inherent repetition and lack of progress toward a thought- or action-provoking conclusion. This formulaic approach to invention and composition is antithetical to writing instruction. If students repeatedly rely on the same simple structure for their written discourse, they fail to experiment with or learn the other options presented as part of each assignment in the course sequence. However, many student writers simply believe that the five-paragraph structure is synonymous with expository writing. You may have to direct students to discover imaginative approaches to composing essays.

Refuting use of the five-paragraph theme structure is easy. Repetition is offensive to an audience, and every good explanation or argument does not automatically fall into three main examples or points. (Usually, in fact, the five-paragraph structure condenses four or five good ideas into three or presents two good ideas and restates them as a third point.) The typical formulaic introduction is neither attention-getting nor particularly interesting, and a redundant conclusion robs the essay of its climax or rousing ending. The five-paragraph theme is just not exciting or intellectually stimulating to write; it is like the five blanks on a typical bank check: date, payee, amount, amount, signature. Regardless of what you're buying, writing a check is always the same and always boring.

Replacing the five-paragraph structure that students find so comfortable can be difficult. It is, after all, adequate communication, and inventing new schemes for every assignment takes a lot more energy than does simply filling in the form. If you discourage use of the five-paragraph theme in class, students may ask you to replace it with another formula. Resist. Encourage your students to discover organic forms for their essays, structures that evolve naturally from what is said. Urge them to let organization grow out of the text rather than imposing form before the text is composed. I ask students to imagine walking around and around the same city block; even if they imagine different parts of the world while they do it, it does not compare with breaking out of their circular track and actually discovering new places to travel. You can help them break out of the five-paragraph mold by assigning short, unstructured writing exercises, such as freewriting or brainstorming. Encourage your students to enjoy discovering what they want to say and how they want to present it.

Research Papers

Occasionally I meet up with bright capable students who are repeating their tenure as composition students because they have balked at writing a course's required research paper. Most departments require at least one research paper during some facet of composition instruction, so you will have the opportunity to familiarize yourself and your students with the library and a good documentation style sheet (such as *The MLA Handbook for Writers of Research Papers*). The research paper is an intimidating assignment, but you can make it less so by allotting plenty of time for library orientation, conferencing and technical instruction on locating research, integrating quotations, determining the validity of sources, and following documentation conventions. I usually allow about three weeks of class time for instruction in my students' first research paper. This is one of the most rhetorically demanding writing tasks undergraduate students must accomplish. It requires the integration of invention and secondary source material into a coherent and persuasive discourse. Still, students need not fear the research paper assignment; writing it is an extension of the same elements they have used to produce essays: invention, arrangement, and style.

Students may find it easier to approach the research paper assignment if you remind them that they are in control. The secondary evidence they will collect is just one kind of proof they will use to establish the validity of their theses. Periodically reinforce the concept that the research paper is an essay whose arguments are primarily generated by its author and reinforced by the opinions and research of other writers. You might allay some of their fears by beginning with a less demanding assignment.

Consider asking for a private draft on a topic each student can really "get on a soapbox" about, or an argument paper in which each student establishes a thesis and invents his or her own main points without consulting secondary sources. Once your students discover that they can generate a substantial amount of content independently, the prospect of searching the library for appropriate reinforcements for their next draft will seem more manageable.

Writing a draft of the paper before going to the library has other benefits, too. It helps students focus their research. Remaining questions and unpersuasive or confusing areas in the early draft can suggest topics for further study. Additionally, a definitive thesis helps students narrow the scope of their research papers. Writers with a specific argument to support will sift through sources and organize their final papers much more efficiently than those making general reports about their topics. Taking a definite stand on the issues and writing a private draft require students to begin with some knowledge of the topic they choose to research. Prior interest and some foreknowledge about the subject are predictors of success with the research paper. Students who try to use the assignment to motivate themselves to learn about an obscure but remotely fascinating topic usually become overwhelmed by confusion and an unreasonably long reading list.

Most first-year composition students will have had no experience with a research library. Even those who felt comfortable and competent in their high school or local public libraries will experience culture shock in the university stacks. Large research libraries hold more kinds of materials than most public libraries do, and they catalog them differently. For instance, my students are amazed to learn that periodicals vastly outnumber books in the university library. Recoiling from the overwhelming amount of sheer stuff in a research library, many students will seek out the familiar card catalog and *Readers' Guide to Periodical Literature* for their papers' sources. Make sure your students also learn to access trade and professional publications through specialized bibliographies and electronic databases (if they are available). Encourage students to ask reference librarians for help. Urge them to seek out library special collections and holdings (government publications; raw research data; rare books and manuscripts; audio, video, and electronic materials; and historical archives). Give them examples of interesting materials that can make the research process more engaging. If your school has a library-orientation program, require your students to attend it. If no such program exists, ask a librarian to meet with your class or take your students to the library and conduct a tour.

Students who are intimidated by the research paper writing process often cite documentation as the most unsettling part of the assignment. You can help them clear this hurdle if, early in the research process, you tell students to take down bibliographic information (for books, for example, the author, editor, title, city of publication, publisher, copyright date, and page numbers) for each source they read. That way, they will be prepared to establish documentation with the first draft in which they incorporate research. Then, when it is time for students to insert documentation and compile a works-cited list, give an overview of documentation in class. In that session, you can assign reading from a research paper casebook, documentation style sheet, or the relevant pages from a composition handbook. Don't present the preponderance of documentation forms in class; that would be like teaching spelling entry-by-entry through the dictionary. Stress that it is not necessary to memorize every aspect of MLA or APA conventions. Instruct students to copy the forms they need from available texts, and demonstrate the wide variety of documentation modeled in the assigned book. Give an exercise from the textbook (or of your own making) to check students' understanding of the documentation process before their papers are due.

Undoubtedly you have written many research papers in your own career. Use the knowledge you gained through experience to help guide your students through the research paper writing process. How do you approach research? Which sources are helpful to you in establishing a working bibliography? Do you take notes in the library, or do you like to check out materials? Why? Do you use note cards? How? Do you take down direct quotations or summarize most of your sources? Which organizational strategy works best for you? You are probably an expert in your own research paper writing process, and you can turn that insight into a teaching strategy. Give advice; offer alternatives.

Abstracts

A student once showed me a handwritten version of Jack Kerouac's *On the Road*. "What is this?" I asked incredulously, since Kerouac is thought to have composed at the typewriter.

"It's mine," the student explained. A teacher of his had recommended that he learn to write by copying a text he admired. I wondered if he thought it had worked. "Not really," he confessed. "After a while words seemed funny; then individual letters seemed all wrong. I forgot what I was copying, and my subconscious just took over." I suggested that he might have replicated Kerouac's *experience* with writing the trip novel but that there are less-monotonous methods for mastering *technique*.

Assigning abstracts that outline, analyze, or condense an established discourse can sharpen students' critical reading skills and deepen their understanding of the composing process. For example, you might encourage students to read prose models more carefully by asking them to compose a one-page summary of the text. Abstracts range from outlines, such as a list of topic sentences for each paragraph in an essay, to rhetorical analyses, in which students identify the intended audience, purpose, and organizational strategy of a text and evaluate its effectiveness. Requiring students to write abstracts of articles that will be cited in their research papers helps them synthesize information. The abstract assignment can be as simple, however, as asking student writers to recount their favorite part of an essay.

Writing abstracts helps students learn to read more closely and critically, and it prompts them to consider some of the rhetorical choices writers must confront. You can teach students to write abstracts by showing them models, composing an abstract of a reading assignment as a group activity in class, or issuing a guide or outline the first time you assign an abstract. Try to demonstrate that a good abstract is a short version, but not a reduction, of the information in the original text. All of the original manuscript's main points should be represented in the abstract.

After students gain some experience summarizing and condensing professional writing, you might ask them to exchange drafts of their own papers and to write an abstract of a peer's essay. At the end of the exercise, direct students to give their abstracts to the essay writers when they return their drafts. Reading abstracts of their own work, student writers often discover discrepancies between their aims and their accomplishments. (See Peer Editing in Chapter 7.) Abstracts not only expose confusing points or logical gaps within the essay but also reinforce good writing; peers are quick to reiterate strong points of argument or good imagery in their abstracts.

Abstracts are also a good place to start if you introduce literature in your class. Ask your students about any book or film they enjoyed, and chances are they will offer you a quick (but maybe not brief enough) plot summary. (I heard so many detailed summaries of Pink Floyd's *The Wall* that when I finally saw the movie in a theater it seemed like a ruthlessly edited version.) When they arrive at college, most students are capable of abstracting literature as plot summary. You can capitalize on that and gradually build in considerations of character, theme, setting, imagery, and other literary conventions through a series of abstract-writing assignments that lead to more analytical essay assignments.

Writing About Literature

Oedipus killed his father for failing to recognize his only son, murdered his mother for having illegitimate children, and still won an entire city with his ability to predict the future. John Keats's "Ode on a Grecian Urn" is about two lusty lovers trapped inside a bottle. In "Crossing Brooklyn Ferry," Walt Whitman expresses his anger with a friend who missed the boat. Everyone who teaches literature in composition class has discovered some amusing misreadings of masterpieces. Whether you choose literature as a prompt for an assignment or teach a course in which students are required to learn the art of writing about literature, it is important to remember that writing is the primary subject matter in a composition class. For those of us trained in literary scholarship, there exists great temptation to turn composition class into a literary appreciation or literary theory seminar, but that is a disservice to our students. It is important that students receive the composition instruction for which they have registered, and students without much interest in literature study should not be left feeling they were misled about the course.

Multigenre textbooks provide a sampling of different types of literature (short stories, poems, plays) from different traditions (American, British, and world literature in translation). If your course concentrates on writing about literature, you might opt for one of these for simplicity and for the opportunity to expose your students to a wide variety of texts. If you have knowledge or interest in a particular type of writing, and the school where you teach permits you to focus the course on that, you might capitalize on your enthusiasm. Single-genre anthologies facilitate a more focused and sequential approach to writing about literature. Students, as a group, tend to prefer those genres which high school classes have best prepared them to study—short stories and novellas, generally. But if you introduce literature into composition class with patience and realistic expectations, you can help students expand their understanding and appreciation of other genres while teaching them to write about previously unfamiliar material.

Literature is a natural secondary subject matter in most composition classes because they are offered within English departments and staffed by English teachers. Composition students, however, represent a wide variety of backgrounds and college majors, and many students harbor the same fear of poetry that their teachers have of calculus. Writing students are easily intimidated by the complexities of literary study. They often feel unprepared to discuss or write about literature. Many believe they lack the aptitude necessary to understand masterpieces or contemporary works. Students sometimes dismiss literature as "boring" or "stupid" because they cannot or do not read it carefully. Don't take their criticism personally, but do take it seriously.

One of my better literature lessons in composition class came about accidentally. After our class discussed William Butler Yeats's "Leda and the Swan," examining sonnet structures, mythology, and sexism, a student wailed, "How will we ever know all of this?" I remembered feeling exactly as he did at that minute; it was during my first semester of British literature survey. I recounted for the class my first several encounters with "Leda and the Swan," remembering my woeful misreadings and convoluted explications that preceded my eventual study of Greek mythology, which unraveled my thoughts. The students laughed at my sophomoric ignorance, confident that they could someday "know all of this" because I had eventually learned it.

Keep your learning objectives concerning literary scholarship modest. One way to do this is by using a reader-response approach, which works well in the composition classroom. Rather than insisting on the latest scholarly explications, you could invite your students to write about their subjective interpretations of the literature. Let them express their admiration for a poem's imagery because it evokes some personally meaningful scene, or accept interpretations of Shakespeare that compare the bard's characters to hometown heroes and family members. One effective reader-response writing prompt for literature assignments asks students to identify which story, poem, or play they liked best; to explain why they liked it; and to try to get their readers to like it, too. If you prefer, you might ask students to tell which literary piece felt most true to life and why they found it so convincing. I remind myself frequently that my secondary goal in teaching literature in composition class is to encourage students to read a poem, play, or story for enjoyment when the class is over or to enroll in a literature class during some later semester.

As you guide them in their in essay drafting, your students can progress from a subjective interpretation of literature to explication. New critical explications are feasible as literary research paper topics; in reading library sources, students find prose models as well as insights into the literature they discuss. Many literary theories currently in vogue can provide new avenues for examining texts. Although they are extrapolated from esoteric work, such as that by Mikhail Bakhtin, Jacques Derrida, Michel Foucault, Julia Kristeva, and Jacques Lacan, they provide remarkably straightforward topics for student writers. Class discussion can produce papers that rely on elementary examples, such as the following:

- Deconstruction—Why does E. E. Cummings use "defunct" to describe Buffalo Bill's death?
- Feminist criticism—Does Henrik Ibsen's language stereotype Nora, in spite of her iconoclastic action in the end of *A Doll's House*?
- Psychoanalytical criticism—How does Biff's disappointment in his father figure contribute to his and Willy's eventual downfalls in *Death of a Salesman*?
- Marxist criticism—What does Shirley Jackson imply about government's role in the family in "The Lottery"?
- New historicism—What light do nineteenth-century newspaper accounts of the funeral train that bore President Lincoln's body West shed on Walt Whitman's "When Lilacs Last in the Dooryard Bloomed"?

Some writing students are capable of a level of literary analysis that destines them for success as English majors or literature minors. Occasionally, writing students will identify a previously unnoticed allusion in a literary text or present an offbeat yet plausible reading of a classic piece. It is not fair to demand great literary scholarship of writing students, but when it surfaces, you can encourage it by helping students to develop their ideas and to organize their papers logically. You can be a good literature teacher by being a dedicated composition instructor.

OTHER MEDIA

Right now you are reading from a book, whose genesis is just what you think it was. It started with an idea, developed in conversations, progressed to an outline, took shape as a series of written drafts, and—through the responses and suggestions of several readers—became the text you now possess. The same general process can result in a number of products, not all of them printed text. Writing for other media is often very similar to inventing and composing an essay or a book. Collecting and reporting news is very much like organizing and writing a research paper. Selling a product incorporates many of the same strategies as writing an argument essay. Interpreting literature through a screenplay requires the same analysis as a literary abstract or review. Our media-rich culture is fueled by a lot of written text that is matched with or transformed into other media. Perhaps you would prefer this text to be a comic book, an audiocassette, a radio show, a videotape, a television series, a big-screen feature film (difficult to imagine), or an interactive computer program. Maybe you and your students would like to experiment with writing in some media other than the printed page.

Incorporating media (besides the printed page) into the classroom can be as simple as asking authors of excellent essays to read their work to the class. Students can perform excerpts of their essays as monologues. In courses incorporating literature and writing, you could assign small groups of students to read from the literary text, breaking it into "parts" and using their voices to emphasize meaning. Investigate the office or department that lends instructional media equipment in your school: Can your students borrow tape recorders, camcorders, video-editing bays, or computer terminals with animation, titling, or video "toaster" capabilities? Use your imagination, and encourage your students to use theirs.

Students can make video "essays" and then write papers analyzing those or recounting the processes involved in producing the videos. For example, video footage of a police officer directing holiday traffic at a local mall, interspersed with scenes from a modern dance performance, provide the basis for a comparison-contrast video essay. Set the traffic-directing scenes to orchestral music and the dance footage to honking car horns, and the comment becomes more poignant. Add the internal monologue of the police officer and the dancer, or of a motorist and dance patron, and text plays a direct role in the emerging film. Portable, easy-to-operate video cameras have had an exciting impact on the writing classroom. Students have the opportunity to write for media that engage their imaginations. In a decade when newspapers and magazines are failing and cable television channels proliferating, multimedia communications seem more relevant to the "real world" than does the printed page.

Incorporating multimedia assignments in your class may be easier if you make contacts with colleagues in media-intensive fields such as film, telecommunications, computer science, theater, or speech departments. You may be able to set up collaborative projects. Composition students, contributing scripts and working with students from other university departments, can produce stunningly sophisticated work in a variety of media. One freshman class I taught became offended by an area business that appropriated a well-known poem for advertising purposes. Believing that the firm's radio advertisements featuring the poem distorted the literature, each student wrote a letter to the company to complain about the ad. We mailed the letters and, when the business offered to send its public relations and advertising executives to meet with the students, the class decided to write new potential ads to demonstrate their ideas. As the students' radio scripts progressed, they needed trained advice and criticism. We turned to a local radio executive and a telecommunications professor for help, and they supplied a professional recording studio and some advanced telecommunications students to act as consultants, directors, and engineers. Eventually actors from another department joined the project, and the result was three nearly professional-sounding radio spots. The composition students contributed many times more energy, research, analysis, and writing than they would have for an ordinary paper, and they were justifiably proud of their product.

Incorporating other media into composition assignments probably excites us all. Spend an hour in a high-tech audio- or video-editing bay and you will have limitless ideas about how to use such great "toys" for creative projects. Some, however, may not involve writing text at all, and media projects in composition class must be an extension or an enhancement of text-producing assignments—manipulating data with sophisticated equipment is not a substitute for writing. All assignments should show students that writing skills are vital to communication in a variety of media.

Some students believe that the importance of writing is diminishing as visual media begin to dominate communications. Writing, however, is unlikely to become an archaic skill or a lost art during their lifetimes. Recently, an international computer network noted that a considerable collection of classic literature, including most of Shakespeare, has been entered into computers and can be downloaded to disk. Our sixteenth-century masters could not have guessed that they would be discussed electronically via satellite, or that their works would spin on hard disks to be read by lasers that can pinpoint any spot in the text in seconds. Text is thought made manifest. It remains humankind's most intricate method of communicating. Perhaps the days of the printed page are limited, but the basic skills taught in today's composition classes are vital to other communications media, now and in the foreseeable future.

Suggested Sources for Further Reading (Part One)

Aristotle. *Poetics*. Trans. S. H. Butcher. *Criticism: The Major Texts*. Ed. W. J. Bate. New York: Harcourt, 1970.

———. *On Rhetoric: A Theory of Civic Discourse*. Trans. George A. Kennedy. New York: Oxford University Press, 1991.

Bain, Alexander. *English Composition and Rhetoric*. London: Longmans, 1877.

Belanoff, Pat, Peter Elbow, and Sheryl I. Fontaine, eds. *Nothing Begins with Nothing: New Investigations of Freewriting*. Carbondale: Southern Illinois University Press, 1991.

Berthoff, Ann E. *The Sense of Learning*. Portsmouth, N.H.: Boynton/Cook, 1990.

Bruffee, Kenneth. "Collaborative Learning: Some Practical Models." *College English* 34 (1973): 634–43.

———, and Kathleen M. Blair. "Two Comments on Computer Conferences and Learning: Authority, Resistance, and Internally Persuasive Discourse." *College English* 53 (1991): 950–53.

Buley-Meissner, Mary Louise. "Nothing Begins with N: New Investigations of Freewriting." *College English* 55 (1993): 211–21.

Bullock, Richard, and John Trimbur, eds. Charles Schuster, general ed. *The Politics of Writing Instruction: Postsecondary*. Portsmouth, N.H.: Heinemann, 1991.

Conners, Robert J., Lisa Ede, and Andrea A. Lunsford, eds. *Essays on Classical Rhetoric and Modern Discourse*. Carbondale: Southern Illinois University Press, 1984.

Corbett, Edward P. J. *Classical Rhetoric for the Modern Student*. 3rd ed. New York: Oxford University Press, 1990.

D'Angelo, Frank. "Nineteenth-century Forms/Modes of Discourse: A Critical Inquiry." *College Composition and Communication* 35 (1984): 31–42.

Davis, Karen. "On the Use of Writing Models in Freshman English." *Teaching English in the Two-Year College* 10 (1984): 211–14.

Donovan, Timothy, and Ben W. McClelland, eds. *Eight Approaches to Teaching Composition*. Urbana, Ill.: NCTE, 1980.

Elbow, Peter. *Writing with Power: Techniques for Mastering the Writing Process*. New York: Oxford University Press, 1981.

————. *Writing Without Teachers*. New York: Oxford University Press, 1973.

Emig, Janet. *The Composing Processes of Twelfth Graders*. Research Report No. 13. Urbana, Ill.: NCTE, 1971.

Enos, Theresa, and Stuart C. Brown. *Professing the New Rhetorics*. Englewood Cliffs, N.J.: Prentice, 1994.

Farrell, Edmund J. "The Beginning Begets: Making Composition Assignments." *Rhetoric and Composition: A Sourcebook for Teachers*. Ed. Richard L. Graves, pp. 220–24. Rochelle Park, N.J.: Hayden, 1976.

Fulwiler, Toby, and Art Young, eds. *Programs That Work: Models and Methods for Writing Across the Curriculum*. Portsmouth, N.H.: Boynton/Cook, 1990.

George, Diana. "Teaching One-to-One: The Writing Conference." *College English* 51 (1989): 418–24.

Gere, Ann Ruggles, ed. *Into the Field: Sites of Composition Studies*. New York: MLA, 1993.

————. *Writing Groups: History, Theory, and Implications*. Carbondale, Ill.: Southern Illinois University Press, 1987.

Hairston, Maxine. "The Winds of Change: Thomas Kuhn and the Revolution in the Teaching of Writing." *College Composition and Communication* 33 (1982): 76–88.

Harris, Muriel. *Teaching One-to-One: The Writing Conference*. Urbana, Ill.: NCTE, 1986.

Hillocks, George. *Research of Written Composition: New Directions for Teaching*. Urbana, Ill.: NCTE, 1986.

Holdstein, Deborah H., and Cynthia L. Selfe, eds. *Computers and Writing: Theory, Research, Practice*. New York: MLA, 1990.

Huff, Roland, and Charles R. Kline, Jr. *The Contemporary Writing Curriculum: Rehearsing, Composing, and Valuing*. New York: Teachers College Press, Columbia University, 1987.

Irmscher, William F. *Teaching Expository Writing*. New York: Holt, 1972.

Kerr, Nancy H. "Linked Composition Courses: Effects on Student Performance." *Journal of Teaching Writing* 11 (1992): 105–18.

Kinneavy, James. *A Theory of Discourse*. New York: Norton, 1980.

Knodt, Ellen Andrews. "The Aims Approach to More Effective Writing." *Teaching English in the Two-Year College* 13 (1986): 30–34.

Larson, Richard. "Teaching Before We Judge: Planning Assignments in Composition." *Teaching High School Composition*. Ed. Gary Tate and Edward P. J. Corbett, pp. 207–18. New York: Oxford University Press, 1970.

Lauer, Janice. "Heuristics and Composition." *College Composition and Communication* 21 (1970): 161–67.

Lindemann, Erika. *A Rhetoric for Writing Teachers*. New York: Oxford University Press, 1987.

Lunsford, Andrea, Helene Moglen, and James Slevin. *The Right to Literacy*. New York: MLA, 1990.

Macrorie, Ken. *Telling Writing*. Rochelle Park, N.J.: Hayden, 1970.

Maimon, Elaine P., Barbara F. Nodine, and Finbarr W. O'Connor, eds. *Thinking, Reasoning, and Writing*. New York: Longman, 1989.

Millett, Nancy Carlyon. *Teaching the Writing Process: A Guide for Teachers and Supervisors*. Boston: Houghton Mifflin, 1986.

Moffett, James. *Teaching the Universe of Discourse*. Boston: Houghton Mifflin, 1983.

———. "Bridges: From Personal Writing to the Formal Essay." Occasional Paper No. 9. University of California at Berkeley: Center for the Study of Writing, 1989.

Montague, Marjorie. *Computers, Cognition, and Writing Instruction*. Albany: State University of New York Press, 1990.

Murray, Donald. *A Writer Teaches Writing*. 2nd ed. Boston: Houghton Mifflin, 1985.

———. *Learning by Teaching*. Upper Montclair, N.J.: Boynton, 1982.

———. "The Listening Eye: Reflections on the Writing Conference." *College English* 41 (1979): 13–18.

O'Hare, Frank. *Sentence Combining: Improving Student Writing Without Formal Grammar Instruction*. Urbana, Ill.: NCTE, 1973.

Reither, James A., and Douglas Vipond. "Writing as Collaboration." *College English* 51 (1989): 855–68.

Rico, Gabrielle Lusser. *Writing the Natural Way*. Los Angeles: Tarcher, 1983.

Rose, Mike. "Plugging in to the Global Classroom." *Educational Digest* 58 (1993): 36–38.

Schwartz, Helen J. "Critical Perspectives on Computers and Composition Instruction." *College English* 54 (1992): 207–12.

Solomon, Gwen. *Teaching Writing with Computers*. Englewood Cliffs, N.J.: Prentice, 1986.

Spear, Karen I. *Sharing Writing: Peer Response Groups in English Classes*. Portsmouth, N.H.: Boynton/Cook, 1988.

Sullivan, Anne McCrary. "Liberating the Urge to Write: From Classroom Journals to Lifelong Writing." *English Journal* 78 (1989): 55–61.

Teichman, Milton, and Marilyn Poris. "Initial Effects of Word Processing on Writing Quality and Writing Anxiety in Freshman Writers." *Computers and the Humanities* 23 (1989): 93–103.

Trimbur, John. "Consensus and Difference in Collaborative Learning." *College English* 15 (1989): 602–15.

Williams, James D. *Preparing to Teach Writing*. Belmont, Calif.: Wadsworth, 1989.

Williams, Noel, and Patrick Holt, eds. *Computers and Writing: Models and Tools*. Norwood, N.J.: Ablex, 1989.

Young, Art, and Tony Fulwiler, eds. *Writing Across the Disciplines: Research into Practice*. Upper Montclair, N.J.: Boynton/Cook, 1986.

Zinsser, William Knowlton. *Writing to Learn*. New York: Harper, 1988.

PART TWO

ASSESSMENT

CHAPTER 4

Course Grading

GRADING SYSTEM BASICS

A colleague once suggested that the role of teacher would be greatly simplified if we just gave all of our students A's for their course grades on the first day of class; then we could pour our full attention into helping students learn, instead of measuring their achievements. Our society is not that idealistic, and the role of the university is not that quaint. Employers, parents, alumni, even students, would not accept this plan. Still, I understand what moved my colleague to propose it. It is confusing sometimes to serve as both mentor and evaluator.

The most difficult days for me as a teacher come near the end of the semester, when I realize that a few of my students will not pass the course. Hope springs eternal within writing students. Perhaps because their teachers have been helpful and encouraging all along, students often expect to receive credit in a course in spite of excessive absences, incomplete assignments, and failing grades. Many students do not see their past performance in class as indicative of their ability or potential, in spite of ample opportunity for revision, tutoring, or development. Students with a consistent record of unsatisfactory work may ask, during the last week of classes, "What grade will I get if I make an A on the final paper?"

One of my most memorable students was an eager young man who put a lot of effort into basic writing class but who was severely hampered by near-illiteracy. He failed to progress into the second semester of the course on his first attempt and, in spite of my protests, requested the same instructor for his second try. Late in that semester it was apparent to me that, without miraculous improvement, he would again fail the required competency exam. I requested a meeting with him to discuss his prospects and options, but before I could speak, he assured me, "I know I'm failing again, and I'll flunk out of school. But that's okay. I'm good-looking, and I play golf really well, so I'm sure I'll be successful in life." I knew he was correct. Years later, when his younger sister enrolled at the university, she looked me up to relay her brother's message: He had gone into recreational-vehicle sales in the South, was making a fortune, and went golfing every afternoon.

We can't give A's to all our students on the first day of class, and most of us wouldn't choose to if that were a serious option. Grades can be learning incentives—rewards that coax the best out of students. (You will probably feel a wave of immense satisfaction when you add a hard-earned A or A+ to the final draft of a student's paper, and that will be nothing compared with the sense of accomplishment the student will probably feel.) College students are adults who require honest and meaningful evaluation of their work in order to make education and career choices. Of course we could provide positive reinforcement and impartial evaluation by some other method (such as personal conferences or new and more or less complicated symbol systems), but none would be as efficient as the long-established tradition of evaluation with grades.

Course-grading methods must be fair, firm, and consistent. Depending on the number of papers, tests, and other assignments required in your class, course grades may be based on relatively many or few individual grades. However, term grades derived from at least six marked assignments or course components usually represent a fair sampling of each student's work. The more individual grades you assign over the course of a term, the more broadly each student's course grade will reflect the entire scope of his or her work. (It also means more work on which you will have to assign grades.)

You will need to specify your course-grading methods at the outset of the term. Students need to know which of their assignments will most influence their success or failure in the course. I avoid assigning points to subjective or intangible elements such as "participation" or "effort." Such factors reinforce the misperception that teachers *give* grades; in fact, students *earn* their marks. You can maintain the appearance of impartiality in grading by deriving course grades from clearly assigned and marked work.

It is helpful to students if, when you present your grading scheme to the class, you demonstrate how you will use it to determine final grades. Will you factor letter grades using a 100-point scale? (Such a scale usually breaks as follows: 90–100 = A, 80–89 = B, 70–79 = C, 60–69 = D.) Will you use a 12-point scale? (This usually breaks as 12 = A+, 11 = A, 10 = A−, 9 = B+, and so on.) Or is your choice a 4-point scale? (In this case, 4 = A, 3.7 = A−, 3.3 = B+, 3 = B, 2.7 = B−, 2.3 = C+, 2 = C, and so on.) Whatever scale you choose, perform the necessary mathematics on a set of hypothetical scores in front of the class. As you do so, explain to your students that each time one of the graded assignments is returned, they will be able to determine their current standing in the course as well as you can. If your school's computing system offers a version of an "electronic gradebook," you can keep records in a program that allows individual students to access their own files. They can monitor their attendance record and check grades as soon as you post them. Some students will still check with you periodically to determine their grades "so far." I have learned that my best response to such queries is to reiterate the method I use for averaging grades without predicting the student's final grade in the course. Projections about grades can be misconstrued as promises. You can avoid misunderstandings if you explain that theme writing is influenced by many variables, and speculating would be useless. Promise instead to practice the grading principles you have established and to be impartial; as much as possible, place the responsibility for achieving and monitoring grades on the writers themselves.

Regardless of the measures you take to deemphasize grades and focus on learning or improvement, students will be concerned with their marks —justifiably so, since next term's registration, or even their continued enrollment in the university or college, may be at stake. I try to make grading standards simple and accessible to class participants so that evaluation does not dominate my relationship with my students. Except for a few extreme cases, I am usually unaware of any particular student's evolving course grade. Often when I pass a former student on campus I greet him or her by name. "I can't believe it," responded a student whose research paper about the restoration of the Sistine Chapel I remembered well. "You still know my name, and I only got a C+ in your class." I was surprised that she remembered the C+.

TRADITIONAL GRADING

Because essay writing is a highly individualized skill, writing-assignment marks and course grades are usually determined by letter grades that are averaged, not "curved" or otherwise compared or manipulated to pit students against one another or to place scores along a perfect bell curve. (In most general writing courses, however, scores naturally distribute themselves over a rough curve, based solely on the law of averages.)

The simplest way to establish a course grading system is, not coincidentally, the method with which you and your students are probably already familiar. It is quite straightforward: Each major component of the course is assigned a grade, and those grades are averaged to determine a mean score. For example, a hypothetical student's grades could be compiled traditionally as follows:

ASSIGNMENT/COURSE COMPONENT	LETTER GRADE	NUMERICAL EQUIVALENT
Homework, reports, presentations	A	4.0
Narrative theme revision	B+	3.5
Process analysis revision	C	2.0
Comparison-contrast revision	C+	2.5
Interview theme revision	A	4.0
Research paper revision	B+	3.5
Total		**19.5**

The sum of this student's scores is 19.5. Dividing that by the number of graded course components (6) reveals a course grade of 3.25, a *B* average.

Because this system is mathematically and logically simple, students can easily use it to monitor their progress in the course. This straightforward method of grading is a time-honored system. Its simplicity is the source of its integrity: It is balanced (grades usually are distributed over a wide range of assignments throughout the academic term) and fair (mean scoring is a viable statistic of central tendency). The traditional method is a good course-grading system on which to rely. In later semesters, when you know which assignments you and the students will want to emphasize, you can implement another method or modify the traditional scheme. It is very adaptable.

WEIGHTED GRADING SCHEMES

Adaptations of the traditional grading method are often called weighted schemes because they emphasize certain assignments, giving them more "weight," or influence, in the determination of course grades. Complex grading structures can be developed from the simple, traditional scheme, allowing for more accuracy and fairness in grading.

To devise a weighted scheme, determine the assignments (such as individual themes or reports) and course components (such as homework, quizzes, or preliminary research assignments) you will use to determine students' final course grades. Then decide on a point value for each. You could, for example, assign a fraction of the course grade to each course element, as in the following:

ASSIGNMENT/COURSE COMPONENT	FRACTION OF FINAL GRADE
Homework	1/16
Reading quizzes	1/16
Narrative theme revision	1/8
Process analysis revision	1/8
Comparison-contrast revision	1/8
Interview report	1/16
Interview theme revision	1/8
Research presentation	1/16
Research paper revision	1/4

If you are more comfortable with percentage-based scoring, you can alter the values slightly and represent the scheme as percentages:

ASSIGNMENT/COURSE COMPONENT	PERCENTAGE OF FINAL GRADE
Homework	5%
Reading quizzes	5
Narrative theme revision	10
Process analysis revision	10
Comparison-contrast revision	15
Interview report	10
Interview theme revision	15
Research presentation	10
Research paper revision	20

The scale can be weighted so that more difficult assignments carry more importance than less demanding ones in determining course grades. A research paper, for example, may be worth many times more points than an impromptu essay. Specific point values can be attached to a wide variety of assignments, ranging from individual homework projects and reading quizzes to revised papers, so that students will know the role each component plays in determining their final course grades.

Many teachers weight end-of-semester assignments more heavily than those issued before the midterm. Such schemes reward improvement over the term and offer incentives to students who do not begin the class with all of the necessary skills. Themes turned in near the end of the semester should best reflect students' achievements because, at least theoretically, class participants should be better writers at the end of the term. Also, in a sequentially arranged course, later assignments should be more challenging and therefore should warrant more emphasis in grading.

PORTFOLIO GRADING

Ancient rhetoricians advised their students to wait as long as nine years between composing a draft and beginning to revise it. Most of our students hope to achieve college degrees in less than half that time, and they can't afford anything resembling the luxury of a decade of maturation and reflection between invention and presentation of their work. Student writers usually draft and revise their work over the course of a week or two to meet the demands of a class syllabus. Portfolio grading is a writing class organization and grading system that allows students to revise their work at varying paces and to determine for themselves when each paper is finished. Portfolio writers have the luxury of putting their work aside for part of the term and the opportunity to reconsider and revise before submitting papers to be graded.

Patterned after the portfolios required of students in other creative fields (such as art and architecture), writing portfolios contain collections of each student's best works, revised and polished throughout the term and submitted for final grading near the completion of the course. Closely tied to the process model for course instruction, portfolio classes are usually taught much as is any other writing course with emphasis on revision. Instructors present theme assignments, examine prose models, encourage peer response or small-group discussion of drafts, offer help with mechanics, and evaluate or mark preliminary drafts or confer with students about their progress. In portfolio classes, instructors have the option of presenting more theme assignments than students are required to complete, allowing students to abandon some of their first attempts and to concentrate their energy on their better efforts. If you used this system you might, for example, have your class examine prose models and strategies for ten different assignments and require students to submit only six or seven finished themes at the end of the term. After the final portfolios are submitted, the class may continue to meet to prepare for a last, in-class writing assignment that allows students to demonstrate the skills they have learned throughout the portfolio process. Alternatively, conferences evaluating the final portfolios may be substituted for class meetings for the duration of the term.

Portfolio writing classes encourage students to judge their own work carefully as they decide which drafts to pursue and how best to prepare those for grading. Instructors in portfolio classes look at drafts in progress, either privately or in conference, and offer suggestions for revision. They usually do not grade papers until the final drafts are submitted—about a week or two before the end of the term. A primary objective of most composition classes is to teach students to write and evaluate their own text independently, and many instructors believe the portfolio method is highly successful in achieving that goal.

There are basically two kinds of portfolios that writing students are required to keep or to submit for course credit. The *working portfolio* contains all freewritings, outlines, false starts, and drafts for each essay assignment. It is a complete paper trail documenting the evolution of the final theme. A valuable record for students and teachers, it provides inductive evidence of each student's composition process. Writers can use this record to discover which of their methods, from invention to editing, are most efficient, and teachers can examine the working portfolio for evidence of effort expended and progress gained.

The *final portfolio* is an abbreviated version of the working portfolio. It contains only the final versions of essays that will determine the student's course grade. Usually very neat and professional looking, final portfolios provide a goal toward which students strive. They are the culmination of several weeks of messy revision, brought together at last as finished documents that reveal only what the authors want their audience to see.

Some teachers collect only the final portfolio from their students at the end of the term, preferring to let the essays succeed or fail on their own merits. Others ask for the entire working collection before they determine course grades, electing to consider all levels of the writing process in their evaluations. Whether you grade the working or the final portfolio, it is a good idea to ask students also to include a cover letter introducing the essays they are submitting. In the letter they should evaluate their own writing process, summarize thematic elements of the collection, and identify their intended audience. Writing this introduction helps students analyze the concepts and skills they have mastered during the production of their portfolios, and reading it will help you to contextualize the collection.

Because portfolio students' grades are not established until the end of the term, this system can be stressful for both teacher and student. Students are often uneasy when their progress and standing in the course are not readily apparent. To abate this uneasiness, some instructors assign temporary grades to drafts of essays during the term. Grading work in progress has two potential faults: It can stall student writers in process because they are willing to accept the interim grade as their final mark, and it can trap teachers by making them feel obligated to issue higher marks on subsequent drafts, even if they are only different—not better. The consensus of instructors who use the portfolio method is that it is better to postpone grading until final papers are submitted.

If you require portfolio submissions and you postpone grading them until they are in final form, it will be important to provide frequent and extensive evaluation in such forms as individual conferences, small-group discussions, and written commentary on specific drafts. Make your grading criteria explicit for each assignment so that students will have an opportunity to evaluate their own work. In addition, when you use the portfolio method you must be impeccably consistent, remembering the advice you have issued and noting students' attempts to follow it. Teachers must inspire the trust and confidence of their students if the course is to progress smoothly all semester without explicit grading. I frequently remind students that we share a common goal of identifying and improving their best work.

The real strength of the portfolio course design is that it eliminates artificial deadlines and permits students to use the whole semester's lessons on every graded assignment. It gives students control over their own work, particularly in deciding when it is finished. But the luxuries afforded writers under the portfolio system create a corresponding poverty in faculty time during an already busy period: the end of the term. Grading a whole semester's paper assignments for an entire class—a full teaching load—during the last two weeks of the term is a very demanding proposition. Portfolio grading is manageable only if instructors keep current with student drafts throughout the semester. Familiarity with the final themes (and one or two sleepless nights) makes the demanding grading of portfolio instruction possible. In general, the mechanics of portfolio grading magnify the essentials of all course grading: familiarity with students' work and progress, maintaining consistency with course objectives and expectations, and sincerity in awarding students the grades they have earned.

CHAPTER 5

Essay Marking

When you collect your mail each day, do you scan through it quickly, searching out handwritten addresses and manually applied stamps? Most everyone appreciates personal correspondence because it contains information concerning ourselves and the people and things we care about. Few students reread their own text when their marked papers are returned to them, but nearly all eagerly scour their teachers' comments, looking for praise, evaluation, and directions for accomplishing the same grade or a better one on the next assignment. Theme marking is a combination of personal and professional correspondence, designed to encourage, correct, and direct student writing efforts.

OVERALL MARKING

Several different learning styles are represented in every writing class, and many of your students will learn better by applying your comments and revising their papers than they will through examining prose models, attending lectures, or collaborating with their peers. There are two parts to most theme marking: comments recorded on the student's text and a final note summarizing the evaluation. Ask students to write on alternate lines or to double-space papers that will be turned in for your comments; you may have quite a bit to write on those papers.

On the text itself, you will probably want to note grammar and punctuation errors; you can accomplish this by a variety of methods. If all your students are required to own the same writing handbook, you can abbreviate your comments by noting simply the handbook chapter and section number that presents applicable rules. Although such a shorthand system will require you to be intensely familiar with the handbook, it is a convenient method of quickly directing students to helpful lessons. A similar method of directing students to applicable handbook sections is using abbreviations (such as *C.S.* for "comma splice" or *S-V* for "subject-verb disagreement"). Some writing teachers prefer simply copyediting their students' work, correcting errors on the text. That method works best for two kinds of students: those who are very competent and make few grammar or punctuation errors in their papers, and those at-risk students who might be frustrated by an overwhelming number of handbook sections to study. The easiest way to mark superficial errors on student papers is to circle them or to place a check mark in the margin of the text near the line in which each problem occurs. This is less invasive in the students' writing process than is editing, and identifying errors seems to help highly motivated learners retain the lesson. However, minimal marking frustrates most student writers, who require more direction in the identification and correction of surface errors.

Mechanical elements of writing are also best noted on the text itself. You might begin with comments on the paper's title: Is it accurate, attention getting, and effective? Identify the paper's thesis. Is it logical, believable, and supported by the rest of the text? Note good and bad features of the paper's organization, development, paragraphing, transitions, tone, and use of various sentence types and lengths. Pose questions when information is confusing or absent. Ask about rhetorical decisions: Why is a paragraph short, a transition abrupt, an example omitted? Tell writers when their work is confusing, tedious, or offensive to their potential audience. Suggest prose models for reexamination, or remind students of class discussions concerning mechanical issues.

Don't forget to react to a paper's content and its speaker. Although they are engaged daily in considering writing rules and techniques, composition students still tend to care more about what their papers say than about how they say it. Focusing on composition alone is artificial; every good writer has something important to tell an audience. Remember to respond to that content as you mark papers. Compliment students on a good idea, agree with a rousing and logical point, express amazement at a surprise ending, question an alarming statistic, or offer sympathy or congratulations at personal revelations. In short, serve as audience as well as evaluator as you read your students' papers.

The final note you append to a marked paper may take more time to compose and write than editing the paper does, and—especially on first drafts or in basic writing classes—you may find that you write more than the author of the paper did. Think of it as personalized instruction; it is time well spent. Do not, however, make your comments longer than necessary; a treatise of about 100 to 150 words usually will suffice. The instructor's note has three primary goals: to offer encouragement, justify the paper's grade, and give direction for revision or further study. Say something positive, but avoid empty compliments about an "interesting topic," "wonderful idea," or "great improvement." Find a legitimate strength in the paper (logical outline, vivid example, strong paragraph, clear sentence structure, exact word choice) and praise that, so student writers can recognize and capitalize on their abilities.

Explain your considerations in awarding the grade on the theme. Cite your (or your department's) published grading rubric and briefly demonstrate how the student's essay fits into that. This exercise assures your student (and you) that the grade is accurate. When a paper's grade is lower than a C, I offer, in my written comments, to meet with the student to discuss his or her next assignment. Be careful when discussing the grade (in your note or in person) that you do not imply that it is negotiable.

Summarize any surface and/or mechanical errors cited on the text. If there are several, note the most serious or frequently recurring problems and suggest handbook lessons or exercises that might remedy those. If you wish to recommend tutoring, you might suggest that in your written comments. If your school has an established tutoring program and you include directions for initiating tutoring sessions, many students will follow up on your suggestion. Look forward. End your written comments with a suggestion regarding the next assignment—a problem to work on, a strength to consider using, a topic-generating heuristic.

When you write on students' themes, stay in the character you have established in the classroom. Use a conversational style. Make it clear that you are evaluating the written artifact, not the writer who produced it. Address each student specifically. Thank one writer for her good contribution to class or to a group exercise. Mention to another that you noticed the extra effort he expended on an assignment. Offer a third student your encouragement or help with the next essay. You must sometimes function as an evaluator, but you can always remain a teacher.

SELECTIVE MARKING

Selective marking of student writing means citing only those errors that legitimately hamper fundamental communication. For instance, instructors who believe that sentence-boundary awareness is of primary importance to clear writing may decide to mark on students' papers no grammar or punctuation errors except sentence fragments, comma splices, and fused sentences. The entire class is thus directed to study and eradicate those problems. By concentrating their efforts on one group of errors, teachers hope for a higher-than-usual success rate at eliminating those problems from their students' writing.

Another form of selective marking involves citing errors on only a specified number of pages in each student's essay. Like spot-check quality-control methods, these marking schemes encourage students to study the errors that are marked and then find them repeated throughout the unmarked portions of their papers. Because major surface errors frequently are repeated several times throughout a single essay, some instructors mark each only once per paper, expecting students to discover the others on their own.

Selective marking systems reduce the number of errors identified on each paper, thereby producing a more manageable list of grammar problems for students to study. In the long run, however, such systems often frustrate students. They cannot be sure that an unmarked construction is correct. Many also believe that every time they master a new concept, another previously acceptable element of their writing is called into question. Most students want the option of addressing all of their errors simultaneously, and they expect a full appraisal of their work with each marked paper.

MARKED ESSAY (EXAMPLE)

As a student, I used to lament the number of papers required of me as an English major, as opposed to the number assigned to my friends in other academic fields. Unfortunately, I did not carry this to its next logical extension. Writing-faculty members have to mark many more papers than do some of our colleagues in other academic specialty areas. Somehow, though, we survive, as we did during our student years. Wearing the soot of midnight oil on our brows, we manage to commandeer as much leisure time as everyone else at the university. Although theme marking is slow and difficult work at first, it seems to get faster and easier each term.

When theme-marking time arrives, many beginning teachers wish they could see samples of the way other instructors approach this task. In the following pages you will find a copy of a diagnostic essay assignment and a student's first draft of the essay, complete with the instructor's comments.

DIAGNOSTIC ESSAY ASSIGNMENT

Topic: Tell why you like your favorite film, novel, TV show, or song. Try to convince your audience to want to see or hear it.

Directions: The paper should be 400 to 500 words in length (that's about three to five double-spaced handwritten pages). Papers usually begin with an attention-getting introduction; present and illustrate one or several examples; and end with a thought-provoking conclusion. Remember that this draft of this assignment will not be graded. We are trying to discover what to expect from each other.

Diagnostic Essay — *Okay, but for the next draft, find a title that fits your paper.*

Rowan Benecke, English 114

Animals are "bred"; humans are born.

Having been raised and (bred) in Africa for seventeen

or so years, I suppose I have a biased opinion in favor

The speech was written by the book's author: Isak Dinesen

of the film Out of Africa. The film starts off with a

narrative speech by the actress Meryl Streep who starts

off with words "I once owned a farm in Africa." The

story goes on to tell of a very wealthy woman who

married a man she never loved, in the hopes that they

would be able to combine their efforts and makes some

profit out of the farming business that was developing

in early colonial East Africa. However, he backs down

This is a bit confusing. You introduce several controlling ideas here. Which will be your thesis?

on their "deal" and leaves her to run the farm by
herself in a country that she knows nothing about, and
whose people are totally different.

The story is packed with all the right ingredients
to make a really worthwhile and interesting film.
There is passion and love, when the rich Baroness
(Meryl Streep) meets the debonair hunter (Robert
Redford). There is also a great deal of action as the
story occurs in the early part of the century leading
up to the First World War.

However, probably the most striking thing about
this movie was the fantastic cinematography.

A hundred years ago, Africa was a very different
place than it is today. The only boundaries and
limitations were those man placed upon himself. The
land was fresh and untouched, and the wildlife were
bountiful and roamed wherever they chose. The film Out
of Africa did a fantastic job at showing an Africa that
Is this redundant?
is fast dying and slipping away, even though it was
Be specific.
made in the last decade. The plains of Kenya and *which species are threatened*
Tanzania are still very beautiful and rich in wildlife,
but the film seemed to capture the incredible peace and

You could focus your next draft on this topic.

abundance of life Africa has. Today man has ripped her

of all of its natural resources and nature has seemed

to take a back seat in the onward approach of man's

progress.

This point of view was a major concern of the

character played by Robert Redford, and he predicted

the plight of the natural beauty of Africa. Through

his eyes, we, the audience, were made to feel the   *Help your readers feel it, too.*

grandeur of Africa and were left to gasp at the sheer

majesty and beauty of the country. But it was not only

the photography that captured the audience and whisked

them away into a world of drama and passion--even if it

was vicariously. The intensely credible acting of

                                          awkward
Meryl Streep, Robert Redford, and all the other host of

supporting actors and actresses, gave the film a

          vague
certain magic quality of its own. The audience became

a part of the passionate romance, the bitter fighting

and turmoil of that period and felt the pain at the

loss of the Baroness' farm.

        M
For many people, they came to know and love Africa

for the first time, through the life of the Baroness,

who came from a totally different culture and climate.

The audience was given a chance to see a small but very

special part of Africa that although ^it^ is slipping away,

is still a major part in modern day life. The film

helped capture the imagination of its audience and

involve ~~them~~ *viewers* in a drama that dips from euphoric highs

to bitter lows, and back up again.

As for me, the film helped me appreciate a new

land I love, even if it does make me slightly lovesick

whenever I have the chance to view it again. *— Infuse the next draft with this emotion. You do write well. Paint your readers a picture with words.*

Rowan,
Your experience with Africa qualifies you to write a unique interpretation of this film. Instead of diversifying your efforts across the movie's acting, plot, etc., focus your next draft on the film's portrayal of Africa. This might be a comparison between the Africa you witnessed and the one presented in the film, or Africa 100 years ago and today.

CHAPTER 6

Essay Grading

Arguably the most stressful part of a new writing teacher's job is assigning grades to students' recorded thoughts, hopes, memories, dreams, and ideas. You will feel torn between wishing to encourage students or win their approval and not wanting to inflate grades artificially or become known as naive or a pushover. Before you return graded assignments to students, you must be satisfied that your evaluations are accurate and defensible. You probably will receive some pressure to change recorded grades, ranging from arguments such as, "Help me; my parents will kill me," to "Gee, until this, I had wanted to become an English major." I will never forget the angry student who stormed into my office shouting, "You cannot fail this paper! I paid $7.50 to have it typed!" Be firm. If you give in to requests for unearned grades, you will quickly develop a reputation that may plague your career with a plethora of such urgent entreaties.

Before you grade very many student essays you will have to decide whether you intend to consider effort, enthusiasm, and improvement or simply want to evaluate the paper as a finished product. Although it is discouraging to award less-than-passing grades to papers that represent hours of research, drafting, and tutoring, it is almost impossible to assess adequately such intangible qualities as effort or sincerity. These are best rewarded with an encouraging word, a verbal or written acknowledgement that, in spite of the outcome, the student has dedicated his or her best effort to the assignment.

The following are popular methods of assessing student essays as artifacts, or finished products. Although subjectivity colors all our judgments, these provide a set of concrete standards against which to measure individual papers. They help to standardize and justify the grades we issue, so that we can monitor our own consistency and show students the criteria by which we evaluate their work.

INDIVIDUAL DECISIONS

College teachers have graded many more student essays worldwide than McDonald's has sold hamburgers. The number of drafts and finished themes that change hands on campuses across America would probably exceed the number of pennies required to obliterate the national debt. All of this commerce has established a sort of gold standard in student essays, a relatively stable fixed mark against which to judge competency in student writing. Students seated side by side in composition class don't usually compete against one another for essay grades; instead, their papers are compared against general expectations for papers written by students at similar levels of education.

Grading papers by the individual method means weighing each essay against itself, taking note of what its writer does especially well or poorly in the theme. Instructors who determine grades with this method usually begin with the assumption that the paper merits a *C* grade. As they read each essay, they mentally increase or decrease that average grade as they encounter each remarkable feature of the paper. For instance, an essay with an attention-getting introduction and a clearly stated thesis may rise immediately to an *A*– in the evaluator's mind, fall back toward a *B* when grammar errors emerge, and sink to a *C*– when the reader notes that some evidence within the paper does not logically support the thesis.

Grading papers by this method ensures that evaluators give close attention to each paper. Since essays pass or fail based on their internal structure, integrity, and persuasiveness, each must be examined rigorously. This method credits accomplishments as much as it censures errors; teachers are reminded to note the triumphs as well as the defeats in papers. However, consistency is difficult to achieve under this system. Evaluators who grade each paper on its own internal merits and deficits must keep in mind a firmly established grading standard. After you have graded several hundred student essays, you can accurately rely solely on your own judgment in determining students' grades.

LIMITER SYSTEMS

Every Olympic high-diver has a perfect score of ten before he or she leaves the springboard. For each, as the cliché goes, it's all downhill from there. Arcing, tucking, and diving toward the surface below, many competitors lose a fraction of a point for a slow response and another for an unpoised limb; more of the perfect score is sacrificed to less-than-ideal form or an awkward entry into the water. A diver's feat is completed when he or she surfaces, already facing the scoreboard, anxious to learn what fraction of ten remains.

Limiter grading systems work something like high-dive judging. Evaluators start with the assumption that every paper will earn an *A*, but as they read through each, they subtract a fraction from the perfect grade for every error and omission. Limiter systems are usually keyed to a specific set of errors, a circumscribed list of minimal expectations, and serious or typical problems. Evaluators watch for specific "limiters" such as those stated in the following set of guidelines.

DEPARTMENTAL GRADING SYSTEM

A satisfactory essay (*C* or better) must have

1. adequate restriction of the topic, focus, purpose, and audience.
2. logical organization of the essay.
3. unified, coherent, developed paragraphs.

In addition, the following errors may limit the quality and, consequently, the grade of an essay because they seriously interfere with clear, appropriate writing:

1. Inappropriate sentence fragment
2. Inappropriate fused sentence
3. Inappropriate comma splice
4. Subject-verb disagreement
5. Pronoun-antecedent disagreement
6. Errors in verb forms and usage
7. Numerous misspelled words

These comprise a manageable list of reasonably important limiters for evaluators to consider. For those learning to identify and correct typical grammatical problems, this is a useful group with which to start.

Limiter-based evaluation is straightforward and relatively easy to justify to students. If you provide your class with a list like the one above and adhere to it strictly, the process should be clear to everyone involved. Focusing on limiters, however, places inordinate importance on error in the composition classroom. Instead of striving to write well, students learn to avoid certain specific problems. At first, that will radically improve their work. After a while, however, you may discover a drawback in the system: The absence of gross errors does not necessarily guarantee quality writing.

In the long run, try to avoid creating a system that values competent but pedantic prose.

HOLISTIC GRADING

Authentic holistic evaluation is also known as ETS grading. Used by the Educational Testing Service as a method of quickly and consistently marking college board writing samples, true holistic evaluation can be performed only by groups of readers who have undergone regimented training and who work under strict supervision, subject to frequent reliability checks. Essentially, it is first-impression rating applied to a specific rubric. The general characteristics of papers adhering to each grade level are listed in a chart or rubric and taught to teams of evaluators who read the papers quickly, determining which level best describes each paper. Generally, all of the papers to be evaluated are responses to the same prompt and were written under identical conditions. Genuine holistic scoring is highly reliable. (Team members whose scores do not conform to those of the majority are retrained or dismissed.) It is comprehensive; the rubric includes many facets of discourse. Because one goal of holistic grading is efficiency, raters usually spend no more than two or three minutes on each essay. That is adequate if only a grade or raw score is required for each essay. In most teaching situations, evaluators also must mark errors and accomplishments and guide future revisions and/or assignments.

Holistic scoring is adaptable to the situation of the individual teacher evaluating student themes. In most cases, you can't benefit from its speed, and, because you are only one person reading each theme only once, you can't test your own reliability as accurately as can groups of trained and supervised evaluators. However, you can draw up or adopt a rubric and rigorously train yourself to apply it holistically. The following criteria were devised by Doug Hunt of the University of Missouri, Columbia, and describe generally accepted standards for college-level writing.

TYPICAL CHARACTERISTICS OF THE *A* PAPER

- The paper never strays from its purpose or mistakes its audience. The subject is focused, significant, interesting, and manageable.
- Not only is the paper correctly organized, but the organization doesn't seem mechanical or imposed.
- Each topical paragraph has a controlling idea, solid detail, and smooth transitions.

- The sentences are varied in length and structure, according to the author's purpose and emphasis.
- The word choice is almost uniformly good. Words are chosen for precise denotation, connotation, and tone.
- Mechanically, the paper is correct except for excusable errors of inadvertence and violations of extremely technical rules.

TYPICAL CHARACTERISTICS OF THE *B* PAPER

- The paper has a firm purpose but may not always affect the audience as the writer expects it to. It is focused and interesting.
- The organization is correct, but transitions are sometimes strained.
- Each topical paragraph has a controlling idea and good supporting detail.
- The sentences are usually varied to suit the writer's purpose and indicate the writer's emphasis.
- The word choice is generally correct. The writer goes beyond the automatic word to find one more precise and effective.
- The paper is generally correct mechanically, though there are some problems with complex grammar and punctuation traps.

TYPICAL CHARACTERISTICS OF THE *C* PAPER

- Though the paper has some interesting parts, the interest is not uniformly maintained. The purpose is not always clear.
- The organization is acceptable, though some parts may be slightly awry. The essay has a clear thesis or principle of organization.
- Each topical paragraph has a controlling idea and some support, though the support is sometimes a bit vague or weak.
- There are very few errors in sentence structure, but the sentences are not varied in length and structure.
- The word choice is generally correct, but the range of words is limited, so that the diction is sometimes imprecise and monotonous.
- Though the paper contains a few major errors, there are mistakes in niceties of spelling, grammar, and punctuation.

TYPICAL CHARACTERISTICS OF THE *D* PAPER

- Only in a few places does the paper find its purpose and audience. Too often it seems an unfocused exercise rather than an interesting essay.

- Some principle of organization is apparent, but it isn't successfully followed.

- The paragraphing is rational, but the topical paragraphs are under-developed—often a series of generalizations.

- Errors in sentence structure are frequent enough to distract the reader but are not pervasive.

- Words are occasionally misused. Attempts to go beyond everyday vocabulary go awry.

- The sentences conform well enough to the grammar of English as spoken by educated but not fussy people. They often fail to conform to written conventions.

TYPICAL CHARACTERISTICS OF THE *F* PAPER

- The paper seems to be a mechanical exercise without purpose or an audience.

- There is no apparent principle of organization.

- There is no apparent rationale for the paragraphing.

- There are frequent sentence structure errors of the gravest sort.

- Words that should be within the range of college students are misused or confused.

- Some errors indicate failure to understand the basic grammar of the sentence.

- Simple words are frequently misspelled.

Although this rubric looks intimidating, you may find that you can internalize it quickly upon use. It seems like a lot to memorize, but you probably have already learned most of it from your own experiences with writing. The rubric is commonsensical. Its categories are parallel, specifying different levels of competency among the same basic elements of rhetoric and composition: audience, organization, paragraphing, sentence structures, grammar, diction, and spelling.

A good holistic rubric provides for comprehensive analysis of student essays, and it concretely specifies the elements of discourse to be evaluated. Distribute your rubric to students before they revise their essays; essentially part of the assignment, it is a list of general expectations for class work. During grading tasks, the rubric serves as a ready reference, helping to ensure consistency. It can also be used to demonstrate the aptness of a paper's grade.

Holistic grading considers the whole paper. Because it does not simply penalize errors, it reinforces all the elements of good writing. Although holistic scoring is often described as first-impression grading, it is not superficial or cursory. Holistic evaluation quickly takes into account many specific elements of an essay which coalesce into a highly informed first impression. It relies on the usual quantification of errors and achievements inherent in grading student papers, but it doesn't let trees obscure the forest. Holistic evaluators can see the good writing they identify.

CHAPTER 7

Other Assessments

PEER EDITING

Probably all of us have swapped papers with a fellow student at some point in our academic careers, agreeing to read each other's manuscript carefully and provide criticism. Regardless of the kind or quantity of problems we might have noted while perusing a friend's text, we discover that the truth is difficult to deliver. We often return a colleague's paper with vague compliments, stuttering out something like, "It was very good . . . very nice. Actually it was good in the nice parts, nice in the good parts. . . . Yes, a very good, err, nice, work in all." This, of course, is a charade—helpful to neither writer nor reader. But the exercise can be mutually beneficial when fellow students have been adequately prepared to critique one another's drafts. Peer editing is an evaluation technique used to train students to become reliable respondents to one another's work. As a controlled exercise, it is an effective learning tool in composition classes.

Over time, most teachers notice a pattern in error correction—in themselves and in their students. The first obstacle in achieving mythically flawless prose is recognizing errors. Before computer spell-checkers (and sometimes since) students complained, "How do I know it's a misspelling if that's how I think it's spelled?" They were right, of course; few people willingly make mistakes or leave them for others to find. (Whenever you think other motorists are admiring your good taste and expert auto waxing, they're watching the belt of your best trench coat, caught in the driver's door, dragging along the highway—an error you certainly wouldn't choose to make.) It's hard to spot our own mistakes, especially in writing. After all, we always know what we meant to say; writers can never fully absent themselves from their texts and become objective readers. That's why students give up on proofreading—it is almost useless to them.

Students can, as you know, find and correct errors in text. Give them a short lesson on, for example, comma splice and ask them to complete the handbook exercises at the end of the chapter. In general, students want to learn; they know that if they could get their lessons down it would make their classes much more enjoyable and satisfying. Given a page entitled "Comma Splice Exercise" in which each of twenty items contains at least one comma splice, I am willing to bet that 90 percent of composition students would get about 90 percent correct. Unfortunately, before the end of the week, about 50 percent of those would turn in a paper flawed by at least one comma splice. It is easiest to learn to recognize errors in an artificial situation—a grammar worksheet, an in-class exercise, or a paper deftly marked by an instructor. It is so easy, and so remote from a student's own writing process, that the transference from such exercises is often minimal.

Peer editing provides a realistic context in which students learn to identify errors in text. Driven by the sincere desire to help a fellow student, peer editors read carefully and work diligently to find and correct problems that might elude them in their own compositions. Most find that errors are more apparent to them in another student's work than in their own and, because peer editing works with legitimate drafts—not contrived grammar exercises—the range of possible problems and their corrections is nearly endless. The lesson involves no rote repetition, so each discovery is memorable.

There are many complex and difficult concepts in rhetorical theory and practice; such terms as *vague, awkward, transition, organization, focus*, and *persuasion* are hard to explain, hard to grasp, and hard to discuss at a level of assured mutual understanding. When I was a student writer, my teachers used to try to show me how to be less vague and to write better transitions, and I thought I understood. But when I became a teacher myself and encountered vagueness and poor transitions in students' papers, I acquired a much deeper understanding of the problems and methods for correcting them. The same learning experience is possible for peer editors. When students see complex problems in real-life writing in progress, and when they help to solve those difficulties, it illuminates similar problems in their own work and suggests methods for correction and revision. Once students have learned to identify and correct errors in a peer writer's text, they are more reliable editors of their own work.

A desirable outcome of composition courses is putting students in charge of their own writing processes. When I began teaching, I thought an instructor's level of self-sacrifice on behalf of the class equaled the level of instruction offered. I was wrong. I devoted most of my leisure time to minutely marking each draft of my students' papers. Their final drafts nearly always represented great improvement. The students felt very proud of their work, some of their papers were chosen for student publications, and I believed I had taught them to write well. As time passed, however, I noticed that many of my former students appeared at my office, requesting that I "go over" papers for other classes. At first I was flattered that they sought my assistance; then I realized that they believed they could not write without my help. I had insinuated myself into their writing process—what a grave disservice.

Peer editing provides a method through which instructors can absent their input from students' drafting processes. Usually before midterm, most classes are ready to begin peer editing. On a day when essay drafts are due, explain your peer-editing procedure. To conserve class time, you may choose to have students trade drafts and take them home for review, but it is safer (and less stressful for the students) if you conduct peer-editing sessions in the classroom. (Papers don't get lost, and you are present to answer questions.) One-on-one paper trades, when two students read each other's drafts, simplify the first peer-editing session, but later in the term you may want to mix things up a bit with three- or four-member groups reading members' papers out loud and providing multiple written peer responses for each. If students determine their own group makeup, you will have to labor to keep them on task. Assigning students to groups usually ensures better productivity. Assigned groups can be premeditated groupings designed to challenge or introduce members, or they can be randomly determined (as simply as by asking students to count off).

Assure peer editors that they are not expected to act as "English Professor for a Day." As participants in the class, they are legitimate members of the essay's audience. In many ways, they are more appropriate editors than are tutors, former teachers, significant others, and other readers whom the writer may ask to comment on a draft in progress. They have been issued the same assignment, learned its attendant lessons, and struggled with the same writing task.

Peer editors are expected to provide an honest, detailed response to the paper they read. They need not know names of errors or propose remedies if they can't think of any. You might urge them to circle elements that seem troublesome or simply to note, "Something wrong here." As much as possible, deemphasize marking grammar and punctuation. Most peer editors feel inadequate in those areas, and excessive copyediting in an early drafting stage can discourage further experimentation. Suggest that students instead indicate what they like, ask questions where they want more details, seek clarification where they are confused, and respond to content wherever they have ideas to add.

Explain that peer editors need not worry about eventual grades in the writing assignment. Because final drafts are not graded on a curve or compared specifically with one another, students should not fear boosting another writer's grade at their own expense. Peer editors benefit as much from graciously offering helpful observations as their recipients do from receiving them. By helping others improve their work, peer editors advance their own writing skills.

Ultimately, the peer-edited paper belongs to its writer. The owner of the essay must decide which, if any, of the peer editor's suggestions to heed. It is each writer's responsibility in meeting course objectives to develop his or her writing process. Writers should not blame the peer editor or the peer-editing process for their decisions.

Peer editing has no hidden agendas. Students need not prove that they are becoming expert in marking college essays. Peer editors should be graded on the degree of completeness with which they respond to their partners' papers. A good way to measure that is with a peer-editing questionnaire. Have peer editors fill out a page or two of questions about the draft they review. Then ask students to give their written responses to the papers' writers so that they can consider the comments while planning the next draft. Require writers to turn in their partners' completed questionnaires with their essay revisions. Early questionnaires should be fairly simple, asking peer editors to describe the draft they have read; questions should concern the text as artifact. Later questionnaires can be more specific and might even ask readers to venture some critical judgments; peer editors may be asked to describe their responses, as audience, to the paper. On pages 84 and 85 are examples of a simple and a more complex peer-editing questionnaire.

TESTS AND QUIZZES

As graduate students, my peers and I were extremely fond of an excellent British literature professor who was a notoriously generous grader of reading quizzes, sometimes awarding as many as ten "extra credit" points to a ten-point quiz. When I had neglected to read the second half of *Clarissa*, I cheerfully accepted the week's quiz paper anyway, hoping to score a few points on cleverness and the professor's largess, thus avoiding full admission of my laziness. Scanning through the list of questions for ones at which I might reasonably guess, I discovered the query: "What was inscribed upon Miss Harlow's coffin?" Stunned, I gasped out loud, "Do you mean she DIES in the end?" Everyone had a great chuckle at my expense—as my hope for reading-quiz points evaporated.

Composition classes frequently incorporate some secondary subject matter (such as prose models, literature, computer instruction, or library instruction) on which students might be tested. Quizzes and other examinations sometimes have a bad reputation among students, who see them as punishment for suspected inattention, laziness, or inability, but tests can also motivate and educate students without threatening them unduly. Most students expect to be quizzed or tested on reading material in college classes, and some will be disappointed if they are not given the

Narrative
Peer Editing

Your name _____

Author of paper _____

Please answer the following questions about the story you have read. Use the back of this page to complete answers, where necessary.

1. What is the story in this paper about?

2. What lesson does this paper teach?

3. What is the most exciting part of the story? At which sentence did you find yourself most interested in this paper?

4. Have you ever had an experience anything like the author's?

5. Which detail most helped you imagine the scene?

6. Is the paper happy, sad, objective, suspenseful, etc.?

7. Does the paper seem to have an introduction, or does it just jump into the story? Which would you prefer?

8. Is the story chronological (told in the order in which it occurred)? If not, can you describe how it is organized?

9. Were you confused by any of the details in the story?

10. What has the author of this paper done particularly well?

Argument Peer Editing

Your name _____

Author of paper _____

Please answer the following questions about the paper you have read. Use the back of this page to complete answers, where necessary.

1. Do you think the audience for this paper is in total agreement, inclined to agree, neutral, or skeptical?

2. How could the author establish an *ethical* appeal? (Does he/she have some experience that lends credibility?)

3. Give a brief outline of the *whole* paper.

4. What is the paper's thesis?

5. Which assertions in this paper could be strengthened through research?

6. Are all points of view in the controversy addressed? What are they?

7. Are you convinced by the paper? What are your other responses? (Were you outraged, offended, amused, confused, inspired, etc.?)

8. Ask a question that this paper might have answered about the topic but did not.

9. List any punctuation or grammar errors you noticed while reading this paper.

10. What has the author of this paper done particularly well?

opportunity to prove they have done their homework. If you don't monitor students' reading with regular class discussion or quizzes, they will probably assume that the assignments are not really important to the course.

Testing for familiarity or competence in secondary course material need not be stringent or complicated. If you test just for basic compliance with the assignment, you can expect to award high marks to nearly everyone in the class. Even if very simple reading quizzes don't account for much of the final course grade, students will probably strive for good test scores and take pride in their achievements. Quizzes on daily or weekly reading assignments provide frequent opportunities for students to demonstrate (and for teachers to reward) sincere effort in the course.

Some teachers subscribe to the theory that every reading assignment should be reinforced with a test. Others believe in more intermittent examination. Research shows that randomly intermittent reinforcement is most effective in inducing students to prepare their lessons regularly. One faculty member I know leaves his testing schedule to chance. He carries a bottle containing five marbles, four black and one red, to class each day. At the start of every class meeting, he asks a student to pour out one marble; if the red one emerges, the students take an impromptu quiz on the day's assignment. When a black marble falls out, he puts it in his briefcase, thus increasing the likelihood of a quiz on the following day.

Short-Answer Quizzes

Advanced students can often be heard in the hallway complaining admiringly about their teachers' "picky" quizzes. The difficulty of these exams, they know, reflects their own ability to read and analyze text. As long as students are passing quizzes they take pride in their level of difficulty, but students in composition class are easily frustrated, even humiliated, by quizzes that require more skill or attention than they are able to bring to reading assignments. In most cases, reading quizzes designed to separate the average students from the scholars are inappropriate in composition class. Tests that motivate students to read all of each assignment or to help students discover the salient points in an assigned reading are most conducive to learning.

The most common type of reading quiz, and the one with which students will have the most experience (positive and negative), is short-answer tests. Usually comprising five or ten questions, short-answer reading quizzes can elicit the most obvious or the most esoteric information about any reading assignment. A quiz is not necessarily good because it is difficult to pass. You will find that broad, relatively simple questions are more difficult to write than specific ones that seek obscure information. Anyone can set out to write a test that is impossible to pass; it is much more difficult to construct a set of reasonable questions that will accurately measure students' understanding of an assigned text.

In writing a typical composition class reading quiz, concentrate on elements of plot and theme rather than concentrating on specific details, quotations, character names, intricacies of subplots, or background information. If, however, you make it clear to students that they are to read biographical headnotes about authors, you may wish to write a question or two about the person who produced the assigned text. Some textbook ancillaries contain preprinted reading quizzes that teachers can photocopy for classroom use. For example, on page 88 is a quiz on Frank O'Connor's short story, "Guests of the Nation," from the *Instructor's Resource Manual* accompanying *The Riverside Reader.*

Another method of generating reading quizzes is one I have used successfully. Even well-read students occasionally miss a point on the simplest quizzes, and some suspect the instructor put that question in to trick students (never mind that it is not the same question missed by others). In an attempt to decrease the adversarial nature of giving and taking quizzes, I have generally stopped writing quiz questions, preferring that the students do it themselves. I usually write the first two or three reading quizzes in the semester to set the tone for those that will follow; then I turn the process over to the students. On quiz day, I arrive early and hand out 3-by-5-inch file cards, instructing students to write one quiz question on the day's assigned reading, along with its correct answer. Students may not consult their books for this exercise; I explain that the object is to write a general question, not a viciously specific one. Next, I collect all of the cards and shuffle through them quickly, eliminating duplicate questions and any containing errors of fact. Then, I sort through the remaining cards, looking for a good distribution of fair questions. This may take three to five minutes, but if they wish, students can use their textbooks to "cram" for the quiz during that period. Finally, when everyone has put the text away and has pen and paper in hand, I read the quiz questions.

Generally, I find that students devise more difficult questions than I would but that no one complains about the level of the exam when everyone has a chance to invent it. Student-written reading quizzes decrease the adversarial roles of examiner and examinee, and they encourage students to read more critically, as they are always on the lookout for a good, comprehensive question. Early in the term, I offer to explain why I have not chosen certain questions, demonstrating the qualities that comprise a good quiz item. Throughout the semester, the quality of the students' questions improves as everyone wants his or hers chosen for the exam (especially since writers are confident of knowing the answers to their own test items). The quiz becomes a class project, and no one wants to be left out.

READING QUIZ

Name _____

Date _____

Frank O'Connor "Guests of the Nation"

1. In which country was O'Connor born?

2. Why did Bonaparte consider his duty guarding the English hostages as useless?

3. How did Belcher ingratiate himself with the woman of the house where the men stayed?

4. What appeared to be Belcher's only passion, which he convinced the others to participate in each evening?

5. What is the subject of the "terrible argument" between Hawkins and Noble recounted in the story?

6. Why do the Irish believe that the hostages must be shot?

7. What role does Noble assume in the executions?

8. What does Bonaparte hope for as the men walk toward the bog where the executions will take place?

9. Who first shoots Hawkins?

10. What do Noble and the old woman do when the executions are finished?

Source: From the Instructor's Resource Manual which accompanies THE RIVERSIDE READER, Fourth Edition by Joseph Trimmer. Used with permission.

Freewriting Quizzes

Instructors can monitor student reading habits in a variety of ways. Asking students to freewrite (as discussed in Chapter 3 of this manual) on prompts that emerge from assigned reading will usually give teachers a clear idea of which students have read the material. Students might respond to an author's thesis, analyze the behavior of a character, provide counterarguments against a writer's assertions, or simply recount the outline of the reading material as they understand or remember it. However, since freewriting is usually not graded, you will need to caution your students that this quiz is measuring only their familiarity with the reading assignment. And, since freewriting quizzes are unstructured, you should have few concrete expectations about the content of student answers. In the interest of fairness, freewriting quizzes are usually graded "Pass" or "Fail," purely on the basis of whether the student gives evidence of compliance with the reading assignment. If the goal in quizzing students on homework assignments is simply to motivate them to read, freewriting is a quick and enjoyable method of checking and rewarding that activity.

Another benefit of freewriting quizzes is the thought they stimulate in the documents they produce. As you know, students often ask that the class "go over" short-answer reading quizzes; the quiz is read and answered orally, with perhaps the interruption of one or two contentions that incorrect answers be accepted on some perceived technicality. Checking short-answer quizzes as a group is generally a waste of class time; if the quiz is a monitoring device and not a teaching tool, belaboring it in class gives it undue emphasis. Freewriting quizzes, however, generate as many different (and potentially correct) answers as there are students writing the exam. Going over freewriting quizzes fosters good class discussion and analysis of the pertinent reading material. You will find that students analyze a topic much more perceptively and articulately if they have the opportunity to freewrite on it first. You may find you prefer routinely beginning class discussion of assigned reading material with a freewriting exercise, followed by an invitation to students to read their freewritings to the class.

Abstracts

Reading quizzes need not be administered in the classroom. Written homework can be just as effective as pop quizzes in motivating students to read assignments. Requiring students to submit abstracts of assigned reading material helps them to distill the text on their own, without the pressure of memorizing details for an in-class quiz. (Abstracts are discussed in Chapter 3 of this manual.) For example, you might ask students to turn in a one-page summary of a prose model, or a prose translation of an assigned poem. Abstracts intended to monitor students' reading can take a variety of forms: an outline, a one-paragraph analysis of thesis, a full-page summary of complete discourse, answers to a list of specific questions about the text, or definitions for a group of words as they are explained in the context of the assigned reading.

Take-home reading quizzes conserve class time and diminish the adversarial relationship that testing creates between teacher and student. They also focus study on the most important details of discourse, which are not always the same as specific, readily quizzed elements. Students who miss questions on in-class reading exams rarely reread the whole assigned discourse to discover their mistakes. In contrast, the added time afforded students by take-home quizzes, and the chance to find every answer before turning in the test paper, allows students the opportunity to reread the assigned text until their abstracts are complete and accurate. While superficial reading quizzes measure students' familiarity with course materials, abstracts demonstrate their level of understanding assigned texts.

Re-creations

You probably enjoy reading and have much more experience with literature than do your students. You may have mentally inserted yourself into the action of a good novel, actually seen yourself on stage while reading a play, or identified totally with the speaker in a poem. It may surprise you that many students have not made that leap into the text. They seem to see literature as a remote artifact because they have not yet developed the skill of reading imaginatively. Much of their difficulty in understanding, interpreting, and remembering the literature they read is due to their distant relationship with it. Re-creations foster a more intimate relationship with text and provide an engaging method of monitoring students' progress with narrative or literature reading assignments.

A popular re-creation assignment is to ask students to rewrite the ending of a story, narrative, or poem so that its outcome is entirely different. A similar task is to extend a story beyond its end, writing about the day following the text's conclusion, or about the remainder of the protagonist's life. If you require students to match the author's tone and style in their re-creations, they will closely analyze those elements of the original text. Students might also rewrite a scene from the assigned reading, literally writing themselves into the action and dialogue, attempting to copy the text's style and to describe themselves and their thoughts as the author might. Another option is having students retell the plot of a story, setting it in another era or geographical place. Re-creation can explode text in a variety of ways. For instance, readers of Edgar Allen Poe's "The Purloined

Letter" might be asked to compose the text of the stolen letter, duplicating its appearance as much as possible and conforming to the writing style and the mores of the story's cultural setting. Or, they might produce a few pages from a character's private diary, imagining what he or she might have recorded concurrently with the action in the story.

Writing a re-creation requires close familiarity with the text, including knowledge of its characters, plot, tone, dialogue, and descriptive details. The exercise engages students in literature, helping them to read more actively. Students learn to absorb the things they read so that they can take them up mentally and manipulate them. As a quiz technique, re-creation is fair to students because it engages their imaginations and allows them to demonstrate which elements of the reading assignment they remember best. Most re-creations are fun to write and amusing to read. Re-creation demonstrates that all writing is fundamentally similar and that it is more accessible than most students believe, since they are able to incorporate their own writing into established text. Once students tamper with a text, they are more comfortable discussing, analyzing, and writing about it. A teaching tool as well as a quiz technique, re-creation demonstrates that assessment can be much more than a test.

Suggested Sources for Further Reading (Part Two)

Cooper, Charles R., and Lee Odell. *Evaluating Writing: Describing, Measuring, Judging*. Urbana, Ill.: NCTE, 1977.

Diedrich, Paul B. *Measuring Growth in English*. Urbana, Ill.: NCTE, 1977.

Elbow, Peter. "Ranking, Evaluating, and Liking: Sorting Out Three Forms of Judgment." *College English* 55 (1993): 187–207.

Faigley, Lester, et al. *Assessing Writers' Knowledge and Process of Composing*. Norwood, N.J.: Ablex, 1985.

Greenberg, Karen L., Harvey S. Wiener, and Richard A. Donovan. *Writing Assessment: Issues and Strategies*. New York: Longman, 1986.

Hill, Carolyn Ericksen. *Writing from the Margins: Power and Pedagogy for Teachers of Composition*. New York: Oxford University Press, 1990.

Huot, Brian. "Reliability, Validity, and Holistic Scoring: What We Know and What We Need to Know." *College Composition and Communication* 41 (1990): 201–13.

Krest, Margie. "Adapting the Portfolio to Meet Student Needs." *English Journal* 79 (1990): 29–34.

Larson, Richard. "Training New Teachers of Composition in the Writing of Comments on Themes." *College Composition and Communication* 17 (1966): 152–55.

Murray, Heather. "Close Reading, Closed Writing." *College English* 53 (1991): 195–209.

Ruth, Leo, and Sandra Murphy. *Designing Writing Tasks for the Assessment of Writing*. Norwood, N.J.: Ablex, 1988.

Shuman, R. Baird. "A Portfolio Approach to Evaluating Student Writing." *Educational Leadership* 48 (1991): 77.

Sommers, Nancy. "Responding to Student Writing." *College Composition and Communication* 33 (1982): 148–56.

White, Edward M. *Teaching and Assessing Writing*. San Francisco: Jossey-Bass, 1985.

Williamson, Michael M., and Brian A. Huot, eds. *Validating Holistic Scoring for Writing Assessment: Theoretical and Empirical Foundations.* Cresskill, N.J.: Hampton, 1992.
Yancey, Kathleen Blake, ed. *Portfolios in the Writing Classroom: An Introduction.* Urbana, Ill.: NCTE, 1992.

PART THREE

CLASSROOM MANAGEMENT

CHAPTER 8

Diversity

Many anthropologists have tried to delineate American social classes in these final years of the twentieth century, and the consensus of several is that a new upper class is emerging in the United States. This new group is defined not by wealth, family name, or other inherited prestige, but rather by its status as an educated or "verbal" class. It comprises, presumably, roughly the same distribution of racial, gender, religious, and other groups now found in our colleges and universities. Today's college students come to school for the same reasons their predecessors did: to get ahead, to make a better life for themselves, and to assume the privileges reserved for those who are educated. These efforts are being undertaken by a more diverse group than ever before.

In part, the changes in campus demographics are the result of hard-fought battles in the U.S. courts and of changing immigration patterns. They also represent a pragmatic, financial response on the part of colleges and universities, which are finding that to remain competitive they must welcome and encourage students from both genders, various skill levels, and all social classes, ages, races, religions, and sexual orientations. As the number of teen-agers across the country takes its cyclical downturn between baby booms, educational institutions—which only recently have enjoyed an influx in applications and entering students—are widening their search processes to fill their campuses each autumn.

The increased diversity in the classroom reflects much more than a savvy response to shifting markets, however. People from various factions of society are being educated (and their cultures are being studied) because of the unique contributions they make to our collective understanding. Our society has long relied on its educated members to lead the way in humanizing our culture, and as our educated classes become more diverse, progress toward acceptance and understanding increases exponentially. We can have an impact on world peace, global understanding and unity, international economics, human equality, and mutual acceptance (or at least tolerance) through the things and people we elect to teach well.

SKILL LEVELS

"Who is Oedipus?" a dejected-sounding young woman asked as I entered the classroom, notes for a lecture on modification in hand.

"Why?" I shot back, wondering how detailed an answer she desired.

"Because someone told me that if I didn't know who Oedipus was, I didn't deserve to be in college."

Oedipus! It would take those basic writing students less than one afternoon to read Sophocles and know as much about Oedipus as most of their detractors. "Let me tell you the story of Oedipus," I sighed, casting my modification notes aside. "It's better than a biography of Elvis, and it starts at a place called Phocis, just outside the ancient city of Thebes. . . ."

Some would rightly argue that the thwarted modification lesson was important to students enrolled in a special writing class, and that Oedipus was better left for Dramatic Literature 101. I agree in principle, but the question demanded an answer and a strong dose of reassurance. I ended the story as *Oedipus Tyrannus* ends, with the blinded king exiled and grieving. I also threw in the exhortation that students really should read the play for themselves; I even hinted at the action-packed sequels, *Oedipus at Colonus* and *Antigone*. At the end of the term, the student who posed the question wrote a passable paper about the correlation between blindness and revelation in *Oedipus Rex*.

We are all better in some subjects than in others, and most of us operate from the isolated pockets of knowledge that education and experience have created for us. I recently joked before an assemblage of Honors College students that I am incapable of balancing a checkbook. A mathematics major in the group later asked if I thought it would be funny for someone to admit the inability to read traffic signs or write a letter. He raised a valid point. Some academic areas are privileged over others, especially in determining who is "college material." In general, we are too quick to equate the ability to communicate verbally (orally and in writing) with the ability to think and reason. As composition teachers, we have the responsibility of helping many otherwise promising students to read and write well enough to succeed in college—in this sense, our task is similar to that of the school financial aid office, which helps learners make up more tangible deficits.

If you teach in a department with different levels of introductory composition courses and a placement system that ensures that students are assigned to the appropriate class, you can be reasonably certain that students on your class list have demonstrated their qualifications for taking the course. However, the typical composition class represents a wide range of skill levels, previous instruction, and writing experience. During the first week of class some students will probably divulge to you their utter disdain for writing instruction, and others will likely mention that they edited their high school yearbooks or aspire to outwrite William Shakespeare. It will facilitate further instruction if you assess each student's writing ability yourself as soon as possible.

A good method of measuring students' writing ability is to begin the course with a diagnostic essay assignment (see Chapter 3). Ask your students to write on a broad topic; a useful assignment for assessment purposes is a writing history—a litany of memorable instruction, achievements, and disappointments. Ask students to chronicle their changing attitudes toward writing and to describe their goals and expectations as writers during their careers as students and professionals. Follow the writing task with individual conferences, and begin by asking each student to recount his or her writing history orally. Listen carefully and note differences between the written and spoken versions of each history. You will probably discover a number of students with plenty to say, yet very few words on paper. Some will demonstrate much greater skill organizing, focusing, and/or developing their story as conversation. Point out these differences to your students. Although you may want to mark and discuss surface errors in these initial conferences, try to focus primarily on the larger issues of writing method, attitudes, and expectations. Assess each student's strengths and problems and work with the writer to formulate goals for the term.

As you make your assessments, you will probably identify some at-risk writers in your class. You may discover students with previously diagnosed or unrecognized learning disabilities (limited cognitive impairments, such as dyslexia or attention-deficit disorder). Ask these students how they have coped with coursework in the past. Chances are good that they and their previous teachers developed methods of instruction that compensated for the disabilities. If it appears unlikely that some students with learning disabilities will be able to succeed in a writing class, or if their problems are persistent or severe, refer them to someone qualified to perform definitive testing: a campus counseling center, an educational testing service, or a school psychologist.

Once you have identified any at-risk writers in your class, you can do your best to help them succeed—within limits. Your impulse may be to offer to tutor those students individually, but resist. You would soon find yourself devoting as much time and energy to that single student as you do to your whole class. Additionally, tutoring one's own students can give them an unfair advantage over their classmates; teachers can become too involved with a text to evaluate it objectively. If your school has an established tutoring center or program, refer at-risk students there immediately, and follow up to make certain that students give tutoring a try. If it does not, you could try to arrange a program informally by soliciting campus English majors and other successful upper-class students to mentor and advise inexperienced writers. There are many different learning and teaching styles, and the methods of a peer tutor may complement your own instruction in such a way that lessons become clearer to students through the combination of your efforts.

Effective teachers do not dismiss their obligations to special-needs students when they refer them to tutors. Keep an open line of communication between yourself and any peer tutors who are helping your students. I have found it especially useful to invite tutors to sit in on class meetings whenever they believe it is necessary; that way, tutors have the opportunity to know, first hand, the expectations for each assignment. Struggling students are not the most reliable translators of class assignments. Remember, it is often easier for you to approach a peer tutor than it is for him or her to come to a faculty member with a suggestion or question. Tell tutors your concerns about individual student's work, and don't forget to congratulate them when you find evidence of their efforts. Don't "dump" problem students on the tutoring center and leave them guessing which miracle to perform for you; work with tutors to make the semester productive for everyone involved.

Unobtrusive methods can be employed in class to encourage and instruct at-risk writers. You may want quietly to schedule an extra conference with a struggling student before an important assignment is due, or you may take care to listen and offer friendly suggestions to a peer-editing group that could use some guidance. If possible, catch up with a frustrated student after class and offer to answer questions (even en route to another class) about the next essay. And, when you assign members for small-group exercises, take care to place at-risk students with others who will offer encouragement and challenge without discouraging them.

Rarely are the poor writing skills of a person admitted to college evidence of low overall intelligence. More often, personal problems are at the root of writing students' difficulties. The inadequate writers in college composition classes often were denied the opportunity to concentrate on developing important cognitive skills because of pressing problems during adolescence—ranging from death or divorce, to physical or emotional abuse, to substance abuse. Many at-risk writers who make the decision to come to college are finally ready to focus their energy on gaining the skills they have missed. You can encourage inexperienced writers by responding to them with respect; they are intellectually competent people. Remember that students cannot compensate for lost years of instruction in a single semester, but they can make some impressive gains. Writing is a process that takes time and experimentation to develop. You cannot give students their own writing processes; you can only offer them the guidance and freedom in which to develop them.

DIALECT AND SECOND-LANGUAGE WRITERS

Language acquisition is a mysterious mental process that begins early in life. Most truly bilingual speakers learned the rudiments of their languages as children. Adults are considerably less successful at learning new languages or dialects, and many retain their native accents with few or no similar speakers in their vicinity. Consider the older people you may have known who speak with a heavy trace of their "old country" or home region in their dialect, regardless of how long they have lived among those who speak differently. It seems that our language patterns become ingrained.

Some of your students will have grown up in communities with social and cultural norms that differ from those they hope to join after graduation. Language or dialect differences will also vary. Some cultures, social groups, and inhabitants of specific regions speak very complex, highly evolved dialects that differ markedly from the mythical standard American dialect generally expected in college writing courses. Different dialects are in no way inferior. Most have evolved from languages equally or more ancient than Standard American English; certain terms and phrases spoken in Appalachia, for instance, are more closely related to Old Anglo-Saxon than are our "standard" equivalents. Unfortunately, it is still safe to assume that employers and other audiences will insist on prose that conforms to standard expectations, so it is a service to students to show them how to write in the manner that is usually accepted in education and business. Do not presume to replace a student's dialect; instead, urge dialect writers and speakers to study Standard American English as though it were a second language. As the "melting pot" simmers through its third century with little sign of cultures dissolving into one another, perhaps it will one day be permissible for people of all cultures to speak and write the language that comes first and best to mind. For now, however, the dominant culture deems it necessary for speakers of other dialects to concentrate on one common language, rather than insist that we all learn to decipher one another's discourse.

Teaching students with dialects that differ markedly from Standard American English can be especially rewarding. Motivated students can make remarkable progress toward learning new speech and writing patterns in a single term. If possible, find a tutor who specializes in English as a second language, one who will respect the integrity of the innate language of nonnative or dialect writers and who will know proven methods of helping such students acquire new speech and writing patterns. Most native English speakers can already hear differences between their dialect and a teacher's. In conference, read dialect writers' papers out loud. They will readily identify grammatical differences when hearing their words in your voice. Use this technique in peer-editing assignments as well; have students read one another's papers out loud within small groups so dialect writers will have the opportunity to discover "errors" before submitting their papers for grading.

Marking the papers of students who write with cultural dialects can be difficult. A lot of the "errors" teachers identify are absolutely correct according to the students' standard usage. Avoid marking dialect differences in the same way you would mark penalized errors. You may want simply to circle problems resulting from dialects. Unless they are handled straightforwardly, corrections can be mistaken for persecution. Meet with students in conference and talk frankly about dialect issues. Assure students that you do not want to eradicate their cultural identity or their language. One minor regionalism in the Midwest is the tendency to begin sentences with the phrase "Being that . . . ." The result is a terrifically awkward construction, and showing students how to convey the same meaning with fewer words will often eradicate such colloquialisms from writing while preserving them in informal speech patterns.

More injurious to prose and more difficult to alter are dialectical speech patterns that do not conjugate verbs, include articles, or organize sentences around independent clauses. Such patterns are common to many foreign students (particularly from some parts of Southeast Asia) and to various racial and ethnic groups in the United States (chiefly African Americans and some Native Americans). These dialect traits are tagged as serious grammar errors and often mandate failure of student themes. It is important for teachers of students with these linguistic backgrounds to remember that grammatical correctness is only one aspect of a student essay. Be sure to look at the essays that these students write, as well as their sentences. Remember that it takes dedication and time to learn a second language, and try to compliment effort as well as achievement. You may find that, in the interest of fairness, you will have to hold dialect and second-language writers to different standards of grammar and correctness, but your expectations for other aspects of their work can equal those established for standard-dialect students. Evaluate skill levels carefully before categorizing dialect writers. Don't assume that because a student appears to belong to a social or cultural group he or she will require or want special attention or treatment. Meet every student as an individual.

MULTICULTURALISM

The factions of our pluralistic society seem to be evolving more interdependence. We now share ethnic foods, philosophies, medical treatments, religious beliefs, literature, common concerns, and political agendas, and, as various cultures within our society interact, more mutual benefit is realized. No longer does the dominant group feign interest in other religions, cultures, and political models out of a mistaken sense of noblesse oblige; every faction of society has something to teach and something to learn from every other one. College students must consider (without prejudice) and employ ideas from various cultures. A multicultural education is not merely the introduction into the curriculum of politically correct representations of other ways of life; it is a general philosophy of education that determines not only what we teach but what we believe and who we educate.

The make-up of college classes is generally diverse, and nearly every group of students includes some minority members. Naturally, we as teachers try to include the works of role models who are representatives of our students' cultural groups, to appreciate the contributions of their ancestors, and to show interest in and value the beliefs and philosophies of their cultures. All students should feel included as class participants, and all have the right to believe that the education they seek is offered to a group that includes them. But we must not limit our multicultural inclusions to the cultures physically represented in our classrooms. The chief purpose of multicultural education is not to make students more comfortable but rather to make them more aware of the richness and diversity of history, religion, thought, and practice available in the world.

Consider carefully the cultures represented in textbooks as you make your selections. Native American, Jewish, African-American, Hispanic, French, and female writers have been part of the American literary tradition since its inception. Other cultures have an even longer history as part of English language discourse in general. Modern multicultural texts often include writers living in other countries, as well as members of American cultural minority groups. With encouragement, most students will display interest in the beliefs and rhetorical strategies of writers from different backgrounds. Trickster tales, for instance, are poignant and humorous, but students are also quick to empathize with arguments presented by contemporary minority writers whose difficulties are not yet dulled by the simplicity of folk tales.

You will be modeling acceptance in your classroom. It is easy to treat text with fairness. Tell readers (when it is not readily discernable) if the author of an essay, story, play, or poem is (for instance) female, homosexual, Asian, African American, Hispanic, or Native American. Ask students to freewrite about the parts of the text with which they identify most closely. Discuss which elements of the discourse are universal and which may be particular to the writer's cultural group. Since most of the selections in textbooks are written for a general audience, don't expect, for instance, that African-American students will respond more favorably or prolifically to an African-American author. If your class incorporates literature, you may choose to include some American classics containing racist overtones (for example, Mark Twain's *Adventures of Huckleberry Finn* and Tennessee Williams' *Glass Menagerie*). Confront these racist statements head on by encouraging class discussion about the society that produced such beliefs. Respond fairly and with an open mind to minority writers and characters in the texts assigned in class.

Because you are a role model for your class, the way you respond to minority students will dictate, to a large extent, the behavior of your students. Of course you will strive to treat everyone equally in class, but you can also show a sincere interest in other cultures by asking students about their beliefs and practices. For instance, you might structure a class exercise in generating a model comparison-and-contrast essay as an outline of the topics of Christian and Muslim rituals. Or you could plan small-group assignments so that minority and dominant-culture students have the opportunity to work together. Lack of knowledge about one another and fear of causing offense are the chief reasons students offer when asked why they segregate themselves in class.

In the classroom, all cultures must cede to the learning situation. Some students will be opposed to female instructors; others may be offended by the diet or religious beliefs of other students. As much as possible, insist on cooperation. One of my colleagues has rightly observed that you can't force-feed tolerance. However, you can help to shape the behavior of your students by demonstrating that it is okay to ask questions about, to disagree with, and even to not understand other cultures, but that it is intolerable to condemn them without trying first to learn.

GENDER

There was a princess who met a nice prince and took him home to meet her family. Her father, wanting to discern the constitution of his potential son-in-law, placed a single pea beneath forty mattresses and bade the prince to sleep there. Dutifully, the prince climbed a ladder and fell into his preposterous bed. The next morning, the father inquired about the sleep of his house guest. "I am a mass of bruises," cried the prince. "My bed contained an awful lump." Should the princess marry this fragile character? Could he be a real prince?

Sex roles are ingrained in us early in life. Even those of us who perceive that our gender has been maligned have great difficulty regarding same-sex peers objectively. We often willingly submit to subservient, second-sex behavior without realizing it, so it is not surprising that we sometimes perpetuate sexism in spite of our assumed enlightenment and commitment to fairness. Although most colleges and universities have flung open their doors to women applicants with an exuberance even Virginia Woolf dared not dream of, men and women are still not equal in the classroom.

Many recent studies of the "chilly climate" in grade school through graduate school classrooms demonstrate that the educations of men and women are not equal in our society. Essentially, these researchers argue that female students are conditioned at an early age to behave passively in school. By various measures, female student participation is demonstrably less than that of their male counterparts. Women also communicate less forcefully in class, more often prefacing their remarks with qualifiers and tacitly or overtly acknowledging the superiority of male opinions. They are less likely to question male authority in assigned texts and are as apt as males to devalue female-authored class materials.

In writing assignments, differences in male and female communication patterns can have marked and damaging effects. Male students are more likely to produce definite thesis statements and to write with a more authoritative tone than are their female peers. Women students tend to produce passive and vague prose in an attempt to avoid offending their audience or claiming too much authority for themselves. Gender roles are learned early and well in our culture, and there is little hope of reversing a lifetime's subtle and persistent conditioning in a semester. Even those who have read the literature on chilly climate find themselves slipping into the old uncomfortable roles many times a day. It may help, however, to discuss the notion of gender roles and chilly climate with your class, urging students to monitor prejudicial behavior in themselves and one another.

Classroom instructors play an important role in controlling the thermostat of the chilly climate. Try to elicit the participation of male and female students equally, and give the same respect to the contributions of women and men. Studies show that teachers cut off or dismiss the in-class responses of females more often than they do those offered by men. Ask your students to help you monitor this tendency and to issue friendly reminders when you slip up. Avoid using sexist pronouns in class. In spite of what grammarians may say, *he* does not refer to females any better than *it* does, and the lack of an animate, non–gender-specific generic singular pronoun is a serious impediment in our language. Also avoid other sexist language, such as comments about students' dress or behavior and jokes at the expense of students or of the cultural or gender groups to which they belong.

Gender biases are so pervasive in society that it is impossible to eliminate them completely—even within the artificial environment of the classroom. The teachers who are trying to eliminate gender discrimination in their classes are themselves usually caught up in gender-inequity issues that pervade the faculty and administration they serve. It is of mutual benefit to all of us, male and female, student and teacher, to work to control the chilly climate—not because it is merely "nice," but because we will all advance when we are all encouraged to contribute equally.

NONTRADITIONAL STUDENTS

One of the most rapidly growing and perhaps most visible groups on many campuses is that of nontraditional students, new matriculates past the typical age of enrollment, students with full-time employment far off campus, or teen-age and older single parents. For many of these students, a college education was simply not an option when they were eighteen years old. Others have taken leaves or dropped out of school to raise a family. Some must work to finance their schooling or to provide for dependents. Still others have recently left their jobs or are seeking to advance longstanding careers. Regardless of which circumstances have prompted their return to formal education, nontraditional students are generally among the most eager and highly motivated learners. Paradoxically, they are also often filled with the most self-doubt and intimidation.

Nontraditional college students frequently require reassurance and reasonable accommodation. During my first semester as a university instructor, one older student was enrolled in the section of composition I was assigned to teach. As soon as I saw her standing at the side of the room, clutching a handbag, umbrella, and rain bonnet, I was terrified. She was older than my mother. How, I wondered, could I possibly inspire her confidence? Would she trust my authority? Almost immediately I was relieved when she waited after class to explain that it had been forty years since she'd had any writing instruction, and she would appreciate any time I could spare to help her brush up. It turned out that she remembered more about writing than she had guessed, but she showed up at my office periodically with questions I could answer comprehensively and authoritatively. I felt somehow that she had ceased to notice the difference in our ages. Then, as she was turning in her final essay on the last day of class, she paused in front of my desk, leaned across, patted me on the head as if I were a pup, and crowed, loud enough for the rest of the class to hear, "Your mother must be very proud of you."

Nontraditional student writers are often besieged by doubt. They may fear that they are not "college material," having been so-judged early in life. They often worry that they have failed to retain important lessons from high school—even if they graduated only three or four years before. They frequently suspect that the younger students resent them, or that the traditional students have advantages resulting from their modern, computer-age educations. In actuality, writing skill seems to be evenly distributed among all students, regardless of age. Most nontraditional writing students will produce adequate or better essays, just as the general student population does. However, nontraditional students frequently recognize the value of college education and seem determined to get the most of every lesson. In general, they are quicker to follow up on assignments and suggestions for revision, and they are more likely to ask instructors for clarification of assignments and remarks on returned papers. It is usually a bonus to find one or more nontraditional students in a class; they often model good "studenting" techniques, present a different point of view in class discussions, and bring a wealth of life experiences to writing assignments. You can add leavening to your small-group class work if you ensure that nontraditional and typical students work together; the interaction is valuable for both groups.

Be sure to include the circumstances of nontraditional students in your course planning. Don't issue assignments or use classroom examples that appeal only to the interests and experience of the eighteen- to twenty-two-year-old set. Remember that few nontraditional students live on campus, and many commute a considerable distance to attend class. Don't give an assignment requiring library work (however little) on Friday and make it due on Monday. If you must cancel class, try to do so in advance of the meeting, so that commuting students don't drive, hire child care, or leave work needlessly. When you require attendance on campus outside of your usual class meeting hours—for a conference or public presentation such as a play, lecture, or film—announce the date at least two weeks ahead of time. And don't offer extra credit for spur-of-the-moment extracurricular assignments unless off-campus students will have the opportunity to participate at home. Even with careful planning, nontraditional students are more frequently caught in conflicts between the class syllabus and work or home life. Try to offer reasonable accommodations. Allow serious students with pressing conflicts to make up work (within reason) and to turn in papers early or late. Insist, however, that all students in the class meet minimum standards of course completion and competence, and grade their work accordingly and impartially.

STUDENTS WITH DISABILITIES

Since compliance with the Americans with Disabilities Act was mandated in 1992, communities, institutions, and employers have worked more diligently to make spaces and opportunities accessible to people with disabilities. Obvious disabilities include those of hearing, sight, and mobility, but less readily discernable problems, such as epilepsy and schizophrenia, are disabilities, too. Depending on the nature of students' impairments, composition instructors may need to make accommodations in course requirements and assignments for these class participants.

Obviously, for example, a student whose vision is impaired would find it difficult, if not impossible, to freewrite or to peer-edit another student's handwritten paper without sophisticated special equipment. Braille typewriters and braille-printing laptop computers make written interaction between blind and sighted students possible. Electronic sound boards enable some students with disabilities to participate in class discussions. In many cases, students who cannot read or take notes for themselves are accompanied by tutors or note-takers who turn pages in books, record class notes, translate lectures into sign language, and verbalize questions for their companions. If your school or department has an administrator specifically assigned to coordinating programs for students with disabilities, consult that person if you think a student in your class requires special equipment or instruction.

Students with disabilities are themselves very resourceful. One need only see a quadriplegic student maneuver a motorized chair through violent weather, into an old campus building, and onto a mechanized chair lift to appreciate that. Most impaired students have encountered physical problems with writing assignments and class participation before, and they either will be able to suggest adaptations and reasonable accommodations or will be eager to work with you to develop alternative assignments and writing arrangements. In general, most students with disabilities are well apprised of their abilities and limitations, and they will tell you when special assistance is required. Some students with disabilities may be more susceptible to illness and hospital stays than your other students, and you may need to allow for this in your attendance policy. Don't, however, make assumptions or excuses for students. Let students with disabilities know that you expect them to let you know when accommodations are necessary. As much as possible, overlook the accouterments of disability (such as wheelchairs, canes, dogs, and electronic aids) and teach the student as fairly and equally as the situation permits. We are not as different as we might suppose. Students with disabilities have been known to refer to the rest of us on our campus as the "temporarily abled."

CHAPTER 9

Course Policies

"I'm sorry, but it's not our policy to give out that information."
"No admittance without identification; it's the new policy."
"Our policy clearly states that you must present documented evidence within three days."

It often seems that policies are rules manufactured at the whim and convenience of powerful agencies, and sometimes they are. Usually, however, policies are an attempt to anticipate problems and conflicts and to ensure that they are managed fairly and uniformly. As you plan your composition course, you should establish a few necessary policies and implement them at the outset of the academic term. Some, such as an attendance policy, late-work sanctions, and penalties for academic dishonesty, should be presented to the students in writing. Others, including your personal policies regarding conflict management or dealing with students' personal crises, require careful consideration before problems arise. Of course you can't anticipate every conflict or unusual situation that will arise in a classroom filled with stress-laden students, but some early preparation will help you react more decisively and impartially if problems and conflicts occur.

ATTENDANCE

Teachers of required general-education courses hear some amazing excuses for absence from class. A first-semester student with little or no experience at diagnosing her own minor ailments called my office once to explain that she couldn't make it to class because she had developed lung cancer. "Lung cancer!" I responded. "Are you sure?"

"Well," she replied, "last weekend my roommate smoked a cigar, and now I have this awful sore throat. What else could it be?"

Attendance in composition class is closely linked to success in the course. It is not a subject for which students can copy one another's notes and still pass the exams. Composition lectures tend to offer many specific options for completing assignments, and class exercises help students invent, organize, and edit their work. Most students take notes in writing class with their own essays in mind; their notes probably will be of little use to their peers. Discussion of reading assignments is often much more helpful to students than simply reading the essays on their own would be. And, because the course is sequentially organized, an extended absence during any part of the term often affects student performance for the remainder of the semester. An attendance policy that encourages students to participate in class regularly will positively influence their achievement in the course. Your first step is finding out whether your department or university has an established attendance policy. Most general attendance regulations leave specific implementation to the discretion of individual instructors. You will need to decide on your own attendance policy before the course begins.

Students who are new to college are often excited about the prospect of controlling their own destiny. High school officials and their parents have, in most cases, monitored their class attendance closely. Perhaps students have heard from older siblings and friends that attendance is not required in college or that students need only show up for tests. Many believe that one component of time management in their new environment is deciding whether to attend classes. Students may expect you to offer an "open" attendance policy, a system in which attendance is expected but not monitored and absence is not directly penalized. An open attendance policy in required general-education courses invites absenteeism. Students assure themselves that there is no penalty for cutting class. Of course, there are indirect negative effects: missed and misunderstood assignments; lost credit for in-class exercises and quizzes; exclusion from peer study groups; confusion, frustration, and defeat from struggling with the course alone. Open attendance policies may foster a degree of self-reliance or measure dependability in more advanced students, and some inexperienced college students will handle such responsibility admirably. Generally, however, laissez-faire policies in first- or second-year composition classes provide a few otherwise-competent students with too much freedom too soon.

Many composition instructors elect to distinguish between legitimate absences (resulting from illness, oversleeping, course conflicts, educational travel, family matters) and illegitimate ones (occasioned by laziness, boredom, and recreational travel opportunities). Such policies usually allow a specified number of unexplained absences (usually one or two hours of class time)—and an unlimited (within reason) number of legitimate excused absences. On the surface, this seems an equitable policy. Students practice responsibility by carefully allotting their unexplained absences, and they are not penalized for factors they cannot predict or control— one of which is excessive illness among those living in the close confines of residence halls, where colds and flu are as ubiquitous as dust motes. However, such complex policies create a great deal of work and stress for faculty members.

An instructor using this system must handle each student petition for an excused absence (and there will be several per day) separately. The teacher becomes a hanging judge—sole jury to each student's tale of woe—every sniffle, complaint, and emergency. Some ask for notes from students' doctors or lawyers or parents before agreeing to excuse absences. Some insist on seeing a printed obituary when a student says a relative has died. That may seem unnecessarily skeptical, but many students feel challenged to take advantage of attendance policies that offer excused absences. Curiously, students who were gravely ill during rush week will be publicly inducted into campus social organizations, or those serving jury duty downtown will return with a golden (fluorescent light-induced?) tan. After a while, you may feel you need Perry Mason's dutiful and accurate investigator Paul Drake to establish the legitimacy of student excuses. Monitoring absences becomes too large a component of the instructor's job if the attendance policy is too complex.

The system of "paid days off" (PDOs) used by many corporations to regulate employee absences is easily adapted to the classroom. In business, workers are granted a finite number of PDOs to use as sick days or vacation time. If an employee is not ill during a given year, he or she has extra vacation time; conversely, every day spent on vacation is a gamble that it won't be needed later in the year as a sick day. Workers manage and allot their own PDOs according to reason and whim. If they misjudge, they are penalized by lost income. However, if they face long-term absence due to serious illness, disaster, or family crisis, they may apply for a personal leave from work, which is regulated under a separate policy.

Teachers wishing to emulate this system can offer students a finite number of hours of absence from class—usually three to five per term— with no questions asked. Students regulate their own attendance, cognizant of penalties for missing more than the allotted class time. Students who overextend their leave time may lose points from the "daily work" or "attendance" part of their course grade. Following absences, students are responsible for collecting missed assignments, notes, and class materials and for turning in work that came due while they were away. Students with special circumstances, who require more leave, can apply to the course instructor for leniency.

At some point, however, absence can prohibit completion of the course. There are many sad cases where student illnesses or injuries or changes in family circumstances prevent students from honoring their commitment to attend class regularly. As you hear the details of these events, remember that your role as a composition teacher is to judge the students' perform-ance in your class—not the legitimacy of the excuse or the direness of the emergency. Granting course credit to a student who has not fully earned it will not compensate for severe illness, disabling injury, divorce, or loss of a wage earner or role model. Encourage students who have not at-tended the course sufficiently to register again when they are better able to give energy and attention to the subject. When students fail the course because of extenuating circumstances, you might also place a letter in their admissions file, evaluating their progress in the course based on available evidence and briefly explaining the situation. That evidence would be weighed in their favor if they are someday able to reapply.

Tardiness is a form of absence that is sometimes difficult to overlook. If you start class promptly, most students will be too shy or respectful to regularly walk in late. However, if some students are habitually tardy, take them aside and ask for an explanation. Chances are that they have diffi-culty finding a parking space, are slow to awaken, must walk a long dis-tance across campus, or come directly from a class where the instructor keeps them late. Explain that tardiness is disruptive and that they may handicap themselves on in-class quizzes or other graded assignments given at the outset of the meeting. If you and they agree that their tardiness is avoidable, ask them to take necessary measures, such as leaving work early, taking a campus shuttle bus to class, setting their alarm ahead ten minutes, or asking the other instructor to observe a more timely dismissal. If the tardiness cannot be avoided, ask the student to work with you by cutting his or her lateness by half. A student who is ten minutes late can probably shave that down to five, and so forth. In truth, the greatest dam-age caused by student tardiness is probably the appearance of carelessness it creates on the part of both students and teacher. Take charge of the situation early in the semester to avoid progressive increases in tardiness throughout the term.

Of course, it is difficult to make attendance mandatory unless you demonstrate its importance in class. Taking attendance visibly reminds students that you are monitoring their participation in class meetings. Model consistent attendance yourself. If you will be away for a conference or other professional absence, ask someone to substitute in class for you. If you are ill, send instructions to the class so that they can continue their work without you. In general, always be on time and ready to begin the lesson. Don't require students to come to a meeting that does not help them with their work. Don't waste their time with irrelevant discussion or with pedantic "spoon feeding" of assigned texts. The best way to guaran-tee good attendance is to teach useful lessons and provide positive inter-action with students in class.

LATE WORK

Hand-delivered by a roommate or friend, mysteriously left at your mailbox, slipped under your office door after hours, or occasionally surrendered by the writer in class, late papers will insinuate themselves into your life. Regardless of how firm, stern, and sincere your policy on late work, some students just cannot get all of their work in on time. Late work is, of course, inconvenient for teachers who want to keep the class moving forward and who detest the persistent drag of incomplete assignments. But it is also unfair to other students who may have compromised the quality of their work in order to meet the deadline. Had they been granted an extra week, or even a day, to polish their essays, they might have located one more crucial source, consulted a tutor, or revised one more draft. You should formulate and articulate a method for accepting late work at the outset of your class. Late-work policies, like attendance policies, function best when they are simple and reasonably strict.

Some teachers refuse to accept late work at all. Under such harsh policies, students automatically fail assignments when they miss deadlines. Although this may motivate some procrastinators to comply scrupulously with deadlines, it more frequently leads to conflict between well-meaning instructors and students with viable excuses for the tardiness of their work. Hard-line positions are, ultimately, hard on their enforcers; teachers who seem inflexible or unreasonable will have difficulty eliciting the cooperation of the class on this and other matters.

A more moderate penalty for submitting late work is to dock its grade, even as much as one letter-grade per class meeting that it is late. Find out if your department or school has an established policy regarding late work; they may mandate or suggest guidelines for determining penalties levied against late papers. Spell out your policy clearly for students, including "gray areas," such as how weekends, holidays, and days between classes are counted (or not counted) in determining the lateness of coursework. When you receive a late assignment, immediately record on it the date and time you accept it, along with the date and time it was actually due; note the penalty that will be assessed against its grade.

Some departments offer a registry for students turning in papers outside of class time. All students submitting work on their own are directed to take it to the department receptionist, who can issue them receipts proving when and where the work was turned in. If a paper is placed in the wrong mailbox or is otherwise lost, the students have proof that they delivered their assignments. Copies of students' receipts are kept on file at the office, and instructors can check the exact submission time and date of late work. A registry system is especially helpful to instructors who are not on campus all day or every day to accept late work.

The best approach to late work is prevention. Try to keep students on schedule because each late assignment detracts from time available for preparing the next one. Composition students usually complete major assignments as a process; they plan and draft their essays long before they are due. Usually, they know ahead of deadline if their work will not be ready. Encourage students to tell you in advance if their work will be late. Offer an extension based on your late-submission policy. You can suggest, for example, that if a paper due on Friday is turned in on the following Monday, it will be docked for only one day's tardiness, but the writer will have three extra days in which to complete it. Occasionally, students will ask for extensions as a result of extraordinary circumstances (such as computers erasing text, libraries failing to supply promised materials, interviewees canceling appointments, and personal problems that are legitimately pressing). You can always privately negotiate your publicly stated policy. Concentrate not on the students' difficulties but on establishing a new deadline that will keep the writer reasonably on schedule with the class.

Occasionally, students whose work has fallen behind schedule will request an incomplete grade for the course. Find out what policy your department has established on issuing incompletes to students in required general-education courses. Some schools simply disallow it. If incompletes are permissible, promise them only to those students you believe capable of completing required coursework in a specified (reasonably brief) amount of time. An incomplete course grade is the ultimate in late work. Students receiving incomplete grades must be motivated and qualified to finish coursework without the benefit of continuing class meetings. Additionally, finishing the previous semester's courses detracts from time spent on the current curriculum. Only in rare cases are incomplete grades appropriate for composition students. Most students who fall seriously behind in writing class would benefit more from another semester in the course. Minor objectives in composition classes often include learning to follow assignments and meet deadlines, and all students should be developing writing processes that enable them to keep pace in the course.

ACADEMIC DISHONESTY

Academic dishonesty, also known as cheating in school, affects us all. It is impossible to determine who is most betrayed by academic dishonesty: fellow students, the teachers, the publishing and academic traditions, or the cheaters themselves. In composition classes, academic dishonesty can take many forms, from copying an answer from another student's quiz paper to accidental misuse of quoted material or full-blown discourse plagiarism. It is likely that you will have to confront instances of plagiarism (both unintentional and malicious) occasionally, but, in many writing situations, you can discourage students from trying to represent others' work as their own by frequently examining work in progress.

Many students are afraid they will accidentally commit an act of plagiarism and be unfairly punished by their writing teachers because they just don't know the rules. Many believe that if they change the original text subtly, they have successfully paraphrased it. Still others believe that certain texts or parts of any discourse are in the public domain and, therefore, are free for the taking. Some think that specific examples, anecdotes, clever introductions, or media in various forms (films, recordings, charts, photographs, computer bulletin board copy) are there to be hunted in a perpetual open season. Like tourists who perennially steal ashtrays bearing hotel insignias and rely on the rationale that it's good advertising for the establishment if its logo is displayed in their homes, students who plagiarize passages from professional writing sometimes believe they are promoting the original writers' ideas—even when they fail to cite those sources. Occasionally, too, quotations that were properly documented in an early draft of a paper surface later as the student's own text, its citations and quotation marks lost somewhere in the recopying process between drafts. In addition, students who receive "help" with their assignments from friends, roommates, well-meaning parents, unofficial tutors, or former teachers sometimes find the distinction blurred between their work and another's input and revisions. As appallingly insensitive or illogical as student ignorance regarding plagiarism might seem, most of it is innocent. Most students do not have the same experience with producing or studying treasured texts that their instructors have, and for them, littering, jay-walking, and failure to license a bicycle or a dog are far more serious crimes than is plagiarism. The first step in teaching writing students to avoid plagiarism is to convince them that it is theft.

I received the first blatantly plagiarized paper in my classes while I was still a graduate student. It was an excellent example of the assigned mode—too good, in fact, to have been written by a first-year student with only a week to prepare it. I asked the student to come to my "office," a surplus desk I shared with other graduate students in the garage of a house annexed as English department storage and office space. Apparently angered by my accusations, and understandably nervous as well, the student flatly denied any dependence on outside sources, insisting instead that she had put extra effort into the assignment. I thought she was a generally honest and capable student, and I was perplexed by the situation. Before I could ask for time to consider the matter, she suddenly sprang to her feet and ran out into a midwinter flurry.

All afternoon, as I continued to mark papers at my well-used and cluttered desk, I watched her, pacing relentlessly on the frozen sidewalk across the street. Finally, as dusk fell in late afternoon, she approached the door. I panicked, then braced myself for the angry tirade I expected. Instead, the student burst into tears and pointed to a textbook left on the desk by another of its assigned users. "You knew," she finally choked out. The essay she had plagiarized was reprinted in her roommate's composition reader, the same one that was on my desk. I had never read the book.

Monitoring freewritings, outlines, rough drafts, peer-editing suggestions, and revisions keeps a teacher very much in touch with students' individual writing processes. When a passage surfaces in a student's draft which obviously reflects a command of the topic, diction, or rhetorical skill beyond that of a student writer, ask to see its source. Although you should present a definition and examples of plagiarism in class, you will probably find that your best teaching on the subject will be the most specific— showing students where they have failed to apply guidelines for citing sources. Whenever you issue an assignment that calls for the incorporation of secondary sources (as in a research paper or term paper), keeping close tabs on students' progress ensures not only that they will be more successful at meeting deadlines but also that they will be less likely to commit crucial mistakes through unintentional plagiarism.

Pandora's box undoubtedly contained the impulse to cheat in college writing classes—or some more generic evil that spawned this insidious behavior. Occasionally—though not as frequently as one might suppose, given the enormous pressure some students feel to succeed in college— students do knowingly, willingly, and maliciously cheat. Usually, you will recognize it as soon as you read it: a chapter from a sociology textbook, the poorly revised version of a friend's B+ paper from last term, or a slick retyped fraternity or sorority file paper. A fully or partially plagiarized essay is almost always easy to spot; its writer may have suddenly and mysteriously changed topics, dropped all of the secondary material from the last draft in favor of older sources, or totally reversed his or her position in the thesis statement. Additionally, the paper probably contains word choices, sentence structures, and ideas or references that are foreign to the writer. It may also report statistics and other research findings without appropriate documentation and may ignore specifically assigned criteria (such as number and recency of works cited). Your initial response will be anger, sadness, amusement, or all three, but if you sincerely believe that a student has deliberately plagiarized work assigned in your class, you have an obligation to deal with it professionally.

Your department or college probably has sanctions regarding academic dishonesty. These may range from failure on the individual assignment, to failure in the course or even immediate dismissal from the university. Usually, however, punishment for a single incident in a composition class is left to the discretion of the instructor, director of the writing program, or the department chairperson. The first step in determining your response to an act of plagiarism is to meet with the student privately in your office. Present your suspicions calmly, and give the student a chance to respond. Most offenders know when they have been caught and will admit their wrongdoing immediately. If not, tell the student you need time to weigh the evidence, and make an appointment to talk again. Suggest that the student gather materials documenting the writing process used to produce the paper, especially if those differ from the drafts worked on in class. If you can locate incontrovertible evidence of plagiarism (the printed source from which the paper was lifted or an identical or significantly similar paper previously submitted by another student), the case is closed; make your decision or turn the evidence over to your supervisor, who will handle the situation.

Plagiarism is often a difficult offense to prove, even though it is relatively easy to identify. If you find no solid proof of plagiarism and the student steadfastly proclaims innocence, even in the face of questioning by a department administrator, apologize and let the incident end. Grade the paper as you would if you had no suspicions. You have not been duped or cheated alone. Plagiarism is a crime against everyone involved: the original author of the stolen text, the other students in the class, the teacher who originated and graded the assignment, the university that grants credit for the course, and, most of all, the plagiarist, who may never learn the skills his or her peers acquired while they wrote their own papers.

MANAGING CONFLICT

As a college teacher, you probably will find that nearly all of your interactions with students will be pleasant: giving friendly advice, answering questions, demonstrating skills, offering encouragement, and providing evaluation. Occasionally, however, you will have to deal with an angry or disgruntled student or with your own frustration over a student's behavior. Most conflict between student and teacher in a writing class, whether over a grade, a policy, or some specific incident of classroom behavior, can be resolved quickly if it is handled calmly and maturely.

Students disrupt a class when their behavior prevents the instructor from giving equal attention to all course participants. Very infrequently, students attend classes when their behavior is influenced by chemical substances or severe mental disorders. If that occurs, the dean of students or a similar administrator should be contacted to facilitate the student's temporary withdrawal from the university. Almost all disruptive classroom behavior, however, falls within the control of individual students and teachers.

The most common form of classroom disruption is seldom recognized as a problem. It appears when students require an inordinate amount of attention and approval, aspire to be the "teacher's pet," dominate class discussion, and, sometimes, appropriate the instructor's office hours. Teaching a whole roomful of students is almost impossible when one of them is constantly the center of attention. Overly eager students usually mean well and often are attempting to compensate for low self-confidence. Take them aside and explain that they must wait until they are called on to make contributions in class. Assure them that you know they are bright, and it is important to give other students a chance to speak, too. I have found it helpful to arrange a "secret sign" with emotionally needy students; it can be as simple as saying their names out loud as I mark attendance. That way, I have acknowledged their presence, even if I don't call on them to speak in class during the hour.

Another kind of conflict occurs when students become irritated with their writing teachers, generally in a dispute over a grade, the specific details of an assignment, or the administration of a policy. For instance, a student may believe she is being unduly punished for missing class if her absences lead to a misunderstanding of a due date, thereby causing her to turn a paper in late and receive a lower grade. Frequently, but not always, when students are unhappy with course procedures or results, they will request an appointment with their instructor to discuss the matter. However, if you know a student is unhappy with some aspect of the class, don't wait for him or her to make the first move. Request a meeting and urge the student to talk about the problem from his or her perspective.

Instructors are usually most disturbed by students' flagrant violations of class policy and classroom order. Students may try your patience by missing class frequently, failing to follow directions for assignments, talking among their friends during class meetings, or creating other distractions in class. Disruptive or defiant student behavior results from many possible causes. Recognize that a few students just do not want to be in college at all. Occasionally problem students confess extreme homesickness, a desire to leave school and pursue some other dream, or a scheme for appeasing parents who demanded that they "give college a chance."

Teachers often feel challenged or threatened when a student expresses dissatisfaction in class. It is easy, as the lone authority with responsibility for organizing, implementing, and assessing class performance, to take criticism of the course personally. Try to gain perspective on the issue. I was once very frustrated by a clean-cut, intelligent young man who audibly expressed disapproval nearly every time I spoke in class. If I said, "Turn to page twenty," he sighed deeply. When I issued an assignment, he would groan.

"Sheesh," he would complain several times each hour. His posture was hostile; his eyes blazed. After about a week, I asked him to meet with me in my office following class. Surprisingly, the chip on his shoulder fit through the doorway, and he showed up on time. I described his in-class behavior, explaining that it was offensive to me and unsettling to his fellow students. He seemed taken aback, surprised that anyone had noticed his mood. He explained that he had fervently wished to apply to West Point, but his teachers and family had offered no support. Consequently, he was at a regular state university, resenting every credit hour of it.

"I see," I ventured, emboldened by his benign revelation. "Well, smell the coffee, pal. You're here, and you'll never go to West Point if you flunk out now. Let's try to have a good semester anyway." He agreed and, once made aware of his behavior, became an exemplary student, one who later might have transferred to a more prestigious school had he chosen to do so.

Of course, every student who acts out in class is not the tragic recipient of fate or family's misfortunes. Defiance in the classroom is sometimes an expression of anger or lack of respect for the course or its instructor. Everyone doesn't teach or learn best by the same methods, and incompatible teacher-student combinations are bound to occur from time to time. Usually, however, only slight compromises are required to make the semester profitable for the student and acceptable for the teacher. Don't ignore expressions of frustration and anger that surface in class, and never return them with similar virulence. Students may express their dissatisfaction with the course by complaining that the subject matter is "boring," the assignment "impossible," or the instructor "unfair." Or they may adopt a more passive-aggressive mode, such as sleeping during class meetings, talking with others in class, refusing to participate in classroom activities, or continually failing to bring course materials to class. Don't try to confront angry challenges or outbursts in front of other students. You may already be feeling outnumbered, as all eyes focus on you, waiting to see how you will respond. Calmly request instead that the student make an appointment to discuss the reason for his or her behavior.

Follow up on disturbing classroom conduct as soon as possible. Ask the student to suggest a convenient appointment time, and negotiate a firm date. If the student does not keep the appointment, hold his or her next graded theme at your office until the writer retrieves it.

The problem student will probably be much more subdued in an office meeting. Explain as briefly and objectively as possible what intractable behavior you have observed and how it affects the class. Ask the student to explain the situation from his or her point of view. Let the student carry the burden of discussion.

When the student has talked through much of the frustration involved in the situation, ask what he or she wants to have happen next. If the requests are reasonable, such as getting an outside reader to regrade an essay or receiving the opportunity to make up a missed assignment, comply. If the student wants an unethical advantage, such as an inflated grade or excessive excused absences, explain why that would be unethical.

Try to end the meeting with a specified plan for the future. Perhaps the student can pledge to attend more regularly, pay attention in class, get work in on time, or ask for clarification or a conference when he or she needs additional help on an assignment. Teachers can volunteer to be more readily available for conferences, put more assignments in writing, review grading criteria with students before essays are due, or give students more choices and more control over future assignments.

Often, a conflict between a student and teacher can lead to a more productive relationship than before. Both may believe they understand the other better after meeting privately to discuss expectations. Occasionally, however, students are not satisfied by such conversations, and their behavior continues to disrupt the class. Refer such students to your department chairperson or the director of the writing program. In general, supervisors don't think ill of teachers who have earnestly tried to resolve conflicts before passing them on. It is best for you and your other students that you not devote too much time or energy to individuals needing or desiring special treatment. As a teacher, your attention belongs primarily to those who are prepared to learn.

Suggested Sources for Further Reading (Part Three)

Adams, Maurianne. *Promoting Diversity in College Classrooms: Innovative Responses for the Curriculum, Faculty, and Institutions*. San Francisco: Jossey-Bass, 1992.

Britton, James, et al. *The Development of Writing Abilities, 11–18*. London: MacMillan, 1975.

Caywood, Cynthia L., and Gillian R. Overing, eds. *Teaching Writing: Pedagogy, Gender, and Equity*. Albany: State University of New York Press, 1987.

Collins, Norma Decker. "Freewriting, Personal Writing, and the At-Risk Reader." *Journal of Reading* 33 (1990): 654–55.

Connors, Patricia. "Some Attitudes of Returning Older Students of Composition." *College Composition and Communication* 33 (1982): 263–66.

Crawford, Mary, and Margo MacLeod. "Gender in the Classroom: An Assessment of the 'Chilly Climate' for Women." *Sex Roles: A Journal of Research* 23 (1990): 101–22.

Dean, Terry. "Multicultural Classrooms, Monocultural Teachers." *College Composition and Communication* 40 (1989): 23–37.

Drum, Alice. "Responding to Plagiarism." *College Composition and Communication* 37 (1986): 241–43.

Enos, Theresa. *A Sourcebook for Basic Writing Teachers*. New York: Random House, 1987.

Farr, Marcia, and Harvey Daniels. *Language Diversity and Writing Instruction*. New York: ERIC Clearinghouse on Urban Education, 1986.

Farrell, Genevieve M., and Peter E. Mudrack. "Academic Involvement and the Nontraditional Student." *Psychological Reports* 71 (1992): 707–13.

Hamp-Lyons, Liz, ed. *Assessing Second Language Writing in Academic Contexts*. Norwood, N.J.: Ablex, 1991.

Kroll, Barbara. *Second Language Writing: Research Insights for the Classroom*. New York: Cambridge University Press, 1990.

Kroll, Barry M. "How College Freshmen View Plagiarism." *Written Communication* 5 (1988): 203–21.

Lunsford, Andrea. "Cognitive Development and the Basic Writer." *College English* 41 (1979): 38–46.

―――, Helene Moglen, and James Slevin. *The Right to Literacy*. New York: MLA, 1990.

Nienhuis, Terry. "The Quick Fix: Curing Plagiarism with a Note-Taking Exercise." *College Teaching* 37 (1989): 100.

Rose, Mike. *Lives on the Boundary: The Struggles and Achievements of America's Underprepared*. New York: Free Press, 1989.

―――. "Nontraditional Students Often Excel and Can Offer Many Benefits to Their Institutions." *Chronicle of Higher Education*, 11 (Oct. 1989): B1–B2.

Shaughnessy, Mina P. *Errors and Expectations*. New York: Oxford University Press, 1977.

Thompson, Merle O'Rourke. "The Returning Student: Writing Anxiety and General Anxiety." *Teaching College in the Two-Year College* 10 (1983): 35–39.

Trillin, Alice Stewart, et al. *Teaching Basic Skills in College: A Guide to Objectives, Skills, Assessment, and Administration*. San Francisco: Jossey-Bass, 1980.

Woodward, Carolyn. "Power, Gender and the Teaching of Writing." *College Literature* 19 (1992): 106–11.

PART FOUR

TEXTBOOKS

CHAPTER 10

Book Selection

How I envied my professors' personal libraries when I was a student. Row upon row of distinguished cloth-bound novels and critical texts lined their offices. The collection of paperbacks I was amassing seemed meager by comparison, and I cursed the luck of being born into a generation that valued convenience and disposability over hand stitching and dust jackets. Later, I realized that scholars' real libraries are in their heads. The books you choose for your students to read will develop the collections in their brains, and the print libraries they eventually gather around themselves will probably be recorded on the media that will succeed CD ROM texts. Choosing textbooks is the task of finding material that will develop students' understanding of the subject in a book that is most compatible with your proposed course objectives and outline.

Many books for composition courses are on the market. In some departments, book choices are made or narrowed down by a selection committee, but many teachers confront the whole array of composition texts as they search for appropriate class materials. Usually, two or more kinds of books are necessary as supplemental materials in a composition class. Separate books present grammar and punctuation lessons, instruction in basic rhetoric, technical writing references, and prose models or literature. Every philosophy, teaching technique, and writing strategy is represented—in almost every possible combination. You may wish to use all the books customarily recommended for composition classes: a handbook, a reader, and a rhetoric. Later, you may choose among them, omitting, for instance, the rhetoric and presenting those lessons as lecture material; or, if you decide to discuss reader assignments extensively in class, you may decide to depend heavily on the rhetoric textbook to supply that component of instruction. If you use all three books for a semester or two, you will discover which best fits your teaching style.

If you have a clear concept of how you want to organize and teach your class, you can search for textbooks that approximate your vision of the course. If you are not dedicated to any one course plan you can browse through available books until you discover a package that seems workable. In any case, it is usually safe to simply "teach the book," that is, to present the course as it is outlined in the texts, chapter by chapter and lesson by lesson. Most composition books are organized in sequential fashion, and, although many contain more material than can be adequately covered in a single academic term, each comprises a reasonably thorough and effective approach to teaching writing.

One of the first things to examine in a potential textbook is its contents. Will the book help you meet established course objectives? If you will be teaching research paper writing, for example, does the book model or examine the process of incorporating secondary sources into essays? Is the book compatible with your own ideas for a syllabus? Do you think its authors have emphasized the most important aspects of the course? Look for the topics and texts you most look forward to presenting; are they there? Do you believe the book's content is accurate? Do you like its examples and selections? Would you be comfortable discussing this material with students or presenting it as a model they should strive to emulate? Look closely at the book's writing; try to read it as if you were a student. Is it inviting, interesting, intelligible, and written at the proper reading level to challenge but not discourage student readers? Will students really read this material carefully?

Consider the book's organization. Is it compatible with your academic term or with the syllabus beginning to take shape in your thoughts? Remember that you need not use a textbook chronologically, but many books work best when they are used in the manner in which they are organized. How much rearrangement or supplementation would be required to match the text to your course plan? If you can't use at least 40 percent of a book, it may not be the right one to ask general-education students to purchase.

Read the book's introduction or foreword and any chapters you would consider controversial or crucial to the discipline. If you seem to disagree with the writer's basic philosophy, you probably should choose a different text. Students are confused when their teachers promote one version of the truth and their textbook espouses another. Don't spend your semester arguing with the book, if you can avoid that.

Besides the textbook itself, which ancillaries does its publisher furnish for teachers who adopt the text? Books may be accompanied by instructor's guides (like this one!), professionally prepared quizzes and diagnostic tests, workbooks, computer software, and other multimedia teaching aids. Such helpful or time-saving materials are not by themselves an adequate reason for choosing a textbook, but they may make a useful book even better.

Consider cost. In choosing a particular textbook, are you asking students to spend more money than it would cost to use a comparable text? Is the book or the course you are planning worth the difference? If the course is important, and you believe a particular textbook is vital to its success, use the best materials available.

Of course it will be easiest for you if you choose books that you can use for more than one semester. That way, you will not have to write a totally new course syllabus each term, and you will be able to review text assignments instead of carefully reading each one as you prepare lessons. No textbook selection is final, however. Books are frequently revised, and new editions supplant old ones. Innovative new books enter the market each term, so keep an eye out for inventive materials and ideas in composition instruction. Choosing a new text from time to time is ultimately a constructive teaching technique; it may prompt you to examine familiar material creatively, and the revised syllabus necessitated by a new textbook can revive a tired subject or teacher. Textbook selection may be an exciting part of your preparation every year or term. Leave yourself time to examine available options thoroughly and to choose books both you and your students will enjoy studying.

REFERENCE BOOKS

Every writing student and teacher needs a dictionary, usually one that weighs at least as much as his or her brain. Condensed or "pocket-sized" dictionaries often omit essential words, definitions, or variations of words. Recommend that your students get a good dictionary, and allow anyone who will carry it to use it while working on in-class writing assignments. I like to let general-education students in on the secret of the confidential source that English-major types use to discover big words, mysterious word origins, accurate pronunciations, and sources of allusions: the dictionary.

Conversely, a thesaurus is one of the few things that is as dangerous in the hands of a student writer as a term-papers-by-mail catalog. Many otherwise competent writers are ruined by their desire to elevate their diction. Unaware that synonyms are not necessarily interchangeable, students frequently substitute words found in the thesaurus for the perfectly respectable Anglo-Saxon terms they know. A sentence such as, "Grandfather's spectacles imbued to him an appearance of grandeur as he descended the vestibule," is typical of thesaurus-influenced prose. Explain to students that consulting a thesaurus for word choices leads to unnatural, stilted, or even nonsensical diction. It is better for student writers to repeat the words they know than to corrupt the ones they don't. If that doesn't work, threaten to "cleave away the auditory apparatus of any pupil appre-hended perusing such an ineffectual tome."

If your course includes a research project, you may want to specify a case book or style manual for students. Case books gather information on a specific topic or instruct readers in collecting material in a specific discipline. For instance, there are case books directed at writers of literary research papers in general, as well as volumes that assist researchers in collecting material on a certain author or a precise literary work. Style manuals provide guidelines both for the preparation of formal research papers and for the documentation of secondary sources. Most English departments instruct their students in using the Modern Language Associ-ation (MLA) documentation style, and nearly every handbook on the mar-ket summarizes that and the American Psychological Association (APA) form in its research section. However, separate volumes that elaborate exhaustively on MLA documentation rules or condense them expressly for composition students are useful in writing classes.

HANDBOOKS

The most accessible way to organize grammar and punctuation conven-tions in standard English usage is to memorize them. Few students (and, for that matter, faculty) have achieved absolute proficiency with the mechanics of their language; most depend on a handbook in the way that savvy travelers occasionally consult a guidebook or phrasebook. College students are reasonably skilled communicators, but most benefit from a handbook that serves not only as a ready reference in solving specific problems but also as a source for comprehensive lessons.

Essentially, the same rules of grammar are presented in all the popular handbooks, with only a few discrepancies between them (such as differing opinions on the interchangability of *that* with other relative pronouns). Virtually all the handbooks offered by reputable textbook publishers are reliable and serve as dependable references and teaching materials in composition classes. However, the books differ widely in terms of overall organization and purpose.

One of the most important distinctions between handbooks is size, particularly as it pertains to scope. Full-size handbooks generally include more apparatus: more detailed lessons, developed examples, and exercises or assignments. Brief editions (some of which are condensed from the longer versions of eminently successful full-scale books) usually cover the same grammar, punctuation, and mechanical rules found in the bigger books, but they include fewer or no exercises and other apparatus. The choice between a full-scale handbook and a less cumbersome edition depends on the uses to which you will put the book in class.

Many students' stereotypical notion of a required English class includes learning to identify parts of speech and parsing sentences. They expect to be bored and frustrated by course content. For this reason, many teachers avoid overt lessons in grammar and punctuation, preferring to teach mechanics through the revision process of students' own writing. Some students, however, believe that their teachers have not attempted to help them with mechanical problems if those have not been explicitly addressed in the classroom. Although college students tend to score well on grammar and punctuation worksheets and exercises, they seem to retain only about as much of the lesson as those who have practiced correcting specific errors in their own work. Therefore, instead of teaching the fundamentals chapter by chapter, you may choose to use the handbook primarily as a reference book, directing students to sections that address problems exemplified in their own writing. If the handbook will be used almost exclusively as a key to correction symbols, a brief edition is probably most appropriate.

Many of the full-size handbooks offer innovative lessons in grammar and punctuation, and some combine the functions of a handbook and a rhetoric text as well. They offer chapters on such topics as invention, tone, audience, organization, development, and research. These comprehensive texts integrate rhetorical and mechanical aspects of writing, emphasizing the importance of both of those aspects of composition and reducing students' natural tendency to agonize over grammar and punctuation issues. Full-scale handbooks are therefore more readily integrated into classroom teaching. Using the handbook in class actively invites students to become familiar with the text's organization and contents and encourages them to consult it as part of their writing process, instead of only when they are directed to correct errors.

Consider the tone of the book you choose, too. Students are frequently intimidated by the subjects presented in a handbook, and an open, inclusive, friendly tone will help convince them that they can master the essentials of competent writing. Grammar and punctuation are inherently prescriptive; avoid texts that sound admonishing. Recognize that any handbook writer who can make the most fussy aspects of an issue such as modification seem inviting is a good teacher to have beside you in class.

Whether you plan to use a handbook as an error-identification and correction resource, a foundation for instruction in the mechanics of writing, or a brief rhetoric text, choose one in which the organization seems logical. The best handbooks are those that are convenient reference tools. You will often want to put your hand on a section quickly during class discussion, in an office conference, or while grading papers; a clearly conceived handbook will allow you to use it efficiently. Choose a book that will work for you; you will, in a sense, be delegating some of your teaching responsibilities to it.

RHETORICS

Rhetorics are, in the strictest sense, *the* textbook for composition classes. Although writing is essentially a "contentless" course, rhetorics provide straightforward, unambiguous lessons in composition subject matter. Everything from how to kick-start the invention process to planning and polishing persuasive prose is included in a good rhetoric text. Most rhetorics are substantial books that can guide an entire course or provide supplemental reading and homework assignments—depending on the needs and course plans of individual instructors.

If you plan to use a rhetoric text as the cornerstone of your class, look carefully at the types of writing assignments each presents and the scope of the course it outlines. Most include guidelines for essays, ranging from chronological narrative forms to expository and research models, and many also include lessons in writing about literature. Choose an edition that supports all or most of the assignments required under your course outline.

Besides large-scale essay assignments, rhetorics also include lessons in the building blocks of composition. Look for useful sections on sentence structures and sentence combining; paragraph organization and development and specialized paragraph composition (introductory paragraphs, descriptive paragraphs, transitional paragraphs, summary paragraphs); critical thinking; and style lessons that encourage the use of figurative language as well as clear, concise clauses.

Consider the tone of the book. In many cases the rhetoric will introduce students to important subjects before you do, and it will stand in for you, answering students' questions when you are not available. Does the book present complicated material clearly without minimizing its complexity? Does it encourage students to try strategies and techniques on their own? Does it make good use of relevant examples and provide concise annotations that draw attention to important points? Is the text accessible? Does it help students quickly locate information they need? Is it up to date? Are its examples current, its facts reliable? Does it reflect recent technological innovations that affect the writing, storing, transferring, researching, and retrieving of text? In short, is it an informed, effective teacher?

A comprehensive rhetoric text usually precludes the use of a separate research paper case book or style guide. Its research section generally follows a research topic from assignment through invention, research, drafting, documentation, and final presentation. The book may also contain sufficient grammar, punctuation, and style sections, making a separate handbook unnecessary. Its examples and prose models may substitute for a separate reader. The most useful rhetorics supply a balanced and comprehensive course in a single volume. You could practically match your syllabus to their table of contents. However, each section or lesson in a good rhetoric is capable of standing alone, making the book a valuable supplemental text as well. It can teach as much of the course as you need it to cover.

READERS

"I sure like the story book," a student remarked one day after class as she tucked the reader we were using into her book bag. "Sometimes I read stuff that's not assigned when I can't sleep." I curbed my impulse to correct her. A college reader is a collection of sophisticated prose models assembled to demonstrate a variety of rhetorical modes, strategies, and purposes. It is a textbook, not merely a hoard of entertaining bedtime stories. Or is it? I remembered myself, gaining early writing education at age nine while reading adolescent detective novels by flashlight under the blankets at the foot of my bed, so as not to awaken my sister. Like most accomplished writers and students of writing, you probably absorbed a great deal of composition instruction from the texts you clandestinely consumed. Similarly, a good college reader introduces students to rhetorical principles subtly, eliciting their cooperation with the promise of a "good read."

As you examine readers for potential inclusion in your composition class, consider the kinds of writing assignments and class discussion you hope the text will support. Most readers are organized either thematically or rhetorically, an orientation that determines not only organization but content. Many rhetorical readers, however, contain a thematic table of contents that effectively reorganizes the book as a topic-centered text, and some thematically arranged collections also list selections by mode or aim. Although a few versatile texts are effective when used either way, most are more balanced and comprehensive in their primary form.

Thematic texts group essays by topic, combining expressive and expository prose on a common theme in each chapter (such as environmental issues, gender roles, career advice, attitudes toward religion, or examinations of social problems). Teachers who present a variety of rhetorical strategies and allow students to determine which form their essays will take find that thematic readers provide a substantial body of common ground for class discussion among students whose individual writing tasks vary widely. Because thematic readers present several points of view on the topics they cover, they can fuel lively class discussion by offering differences of opinion expressed by anthologized authors.

Rhetorically arranged readers provide the foundation for modes- or genre-based instruction. Chapters group essays according to type, such as narrative, descriptive, comparison-and-contrast, definition, and argumentative writing. Teachers who assign aims- or modes-centered composition tasks find that the writing strategy lessons they present are reinforced by rhetorically arranged readers. The books model various approaches to the same specific writing assignment, and the readings can both facilitate in-class discussions of rhetorical strategies and encourage debates over themes and content.

Regardless of their thematic or rhetorical orientation, good readers share a number of important qualities. The best offer a wide variety of selections, encompassing an assortment of topics, authors, rhetorical strategies, and points of view. Look for a book that includes a good mix of classic writers (such as George Orwell, Virginia Woolf, Mark Twain, Eudora Welty, and Martin Luther King, Jr.) and contemporary voices. Examine the book's publication acknowledgements to discover the sources of reprinted essays, and give preference to texts that gather essays or excerpts from reputable publications. Consider the book's multicultural offerings—not only in its topics but in its writers. Are the works of minority authors included throughout the book, and do their contributions address subjects other than "minority issues?" In short, is the book a reliable and accurate representation of the culture it claims to represent? Does it realistically exemplify the discourse of contemporary educated society?

From a pedagogical standpoint, consider how the text supports the students' writing process. Does the book suggest discussion questions for each essay, and do those questions promote consideration of the students' own writing situation? Does the book's content clearly support the course's primary objectives, and are reading assignments obviously related to students' writing tasks? Does the book contain works that students can and will read? The best texts appeal to readers and writers of differing skill levels. For instance, editors might arrange essays hierarchically within each chapter, starting with shorter, lighter, easier-to-read pieces and progressing to more technically sophisticated work. Check to see whether the reader offers a good match between skill level and ability of students. Good prose models encourage and inspire students to emulate them; they must surpass the students' abilities but not their goals. Easily readable essays that fail to entice students are insulting, and fascinating topics discussed on an esoteric plane are frustrating to students who can neither read nor write with such intellectual acuity. It is a real challenge to find a book that students turn to when they can't sleep, but that should always be our goal in selecting readers.

LITERATURE ANTHOLOGIES

It is technically possible that there are more literature anthologies in the world today than there are original pieces of literature, especially since many of them reprint the same literary masterpieces again and again. Sometimes it actually seems there are too many—usually when you must sift through them in search of one to use in composition classes. So many literature books exist to meet the needs of a demanding market; obviously and primarily, they provide subject matter for literature courses of all types, but they also supply secondary material for cultural studies, creative writing, composition, and a wide array of university classes. If you are assigned to teach a course in which students are required to write about literature, you will want to think carefully before deciding on the literature you present and the kind of textbook or anthology you select.

The most popular literature books used in composition classes are differentiated by their content or focus. Large, multigenre anthologies dominate the market because they provide a sampling of poetry, drama, and short fiction, all within one (usually reasonably priced) volume. There is a remarkable sameness about many of the big anthologies which is dictated by tradition and budget. The whole debate about canon is a series of questions and arguments in which you are undoubtedly mired already. Briefly, it considers the notion of whether various literary subjects (for example, modern drama) necessitate the inclusion of certain subgenres (such as absurdist theater) in their study. It even considers whether specific authors and works (like Samuel Beckett's *Waiting for Godot*) must be in-cluded—even at the cost of eliminating more recent or exemplary samples —in order to cover the subject properly.

For a long time, the preeminence of the accepted canon was assumed. No one seemed to question the presumption that a course in British poetry, for instance, was illegitimate unless it included *Beowulf*, the best-known sonnets by Shakespeare, and Keats' "Ode on a Grecian Urn," to name significant but few examples. Furthermore, the inclusion of lesser-known historical or modern figures was believed to dilute or detract from the established canon. Textbooks adhered to the accepted body of works; British poetry and other genres were synonymous with the contents of the anthologies. More recently, teachers have begun to alter the canon, eliminating "must read" pieces from their syllabi and introducing new or previously dismissed authors and works. Anthologies have tried to keep pace with or to lead those changes. The revolution is imperfect, however, because most of the works protected by the old canon are worthy of study in their own right. No one really wants Shakespeare or any of the legions of other classic authors to be forgotten or to be diminished in the minds of future readers. Furthermore, everyone has a difficult time agreeing whether revered authors should be replaced with new literary icons or whether the whole concept of canon can or should be abandoned.

Grand-scale literary anthologies are caught in the middle of this debate. They must continue to publish the established canon for those instructors who prefer to adhere to a classic curriculum—and for those who reject it; one cannot eschew options that no longer exist, so the established canon must stand to be defied. Most recent anthologies reflect changes in the curriculum by including more selections by writers who represent racial and cultural minorities or whose work is experimental or marginalized. Nevertheless, these anthologies are bound by the same old canon, which is not only popular but expedient: A majority of works in the standard curriculum have outlasted their authors' copyrights and are free for the reprinting—they are in the public domain.

Single-genre volumes exhibit a similar sameness from one book to the next, especially among the lower-priced texts. Certain classic plays, poems, and short stories recur throughout the most popular specific anthologies. Some new books, however, attempt to present new voices or contemporary work. Anthologies that collect writing by members of various political, minority, or age groups offer an alternative (albeit a narrow one) to the familiar canon.

The decisions involved in organizing a course in writing about literature will help narrow the field of potential textbooks you might choose. In deciding which genre(s) to study in your class, first determine whether your department requires a multigenre approach. Multigenre courses can be taught using a group of single-genre texts, but the cost of such an arrangement is often prohibitive, especially in a class where students will be required to purchase other writing books in addition to literature texts. If you can focus on one or two genres, consider capitalizing on your own areas of expertise. Students may not think they like poetry, for instance, but if you are knowledgeable and enthusiastic about it, you might change their minds. Consider, too, any outside opportunities available on campus or in your area. Perhaps your students can read a play that the drama department will produce during the term or study the work of an author who will be artist-in-residence or will be reading somewhere nearby.

Once you have determined the genre(s) your class will analyze, you should decide the emphasis literature will have in your composition class. Although improving students' writing skills will probably be the primary learning objective in the course, some secondary objectives may include educating students about a specific literary genre or tradition, or cultivating their appreciation for literature or other points of view. If literature is very important in your course plan, you will probably want to select an anthology that offers students a wide range of reading assignments. However, if the class is first and always a course in writing instruction, you may want to consider a literature text specifically designed for composition classes, one that includes case book analyses of literary texts and assistance with writing assignments.

Anthologies in general contain a varying amount of scholarly apparatus. Decide whether technical terms and concepts are important to your students' examination of literature, and whether you want to introduce extraneous information (such as cultural/historical contexts for pieces, literary terms and conventions, or interpretative data). A good anthology selection will include biographical and/or critical headnotes describing each author and work, footnotes (where necessary) to clarify allusions and archaic or esoteric diction, and a glossary or some other chapters or appendixes that aid student writers in learning to discuss literature. Most important, it will contain a variety of selections that are appealing to students, that you are comfortable teaching, and that meet the course objectives for literary education. Look, too, for individual pieces alluding to others in the book or treating the same subject differently—works that lend themselves to student-writing topics. Plan to teach the literature you love best, the plot twists, ingenious characterizations, well-turned phrases, perfect symbols, and enduring themes that led to the moment where you stand, literature book in hand, before your own students who are encountering all this richness for the first time.

APPENDIX A

Sample Syllabi

ENGLISH 101

Instructor: Rebecca Rickly
Office: RB 249
Office hours: MWF 10:00–11:00 (and by appointment)
Phone: 555-8386
Home phone: 555-8023

Materials Required

Handout packet (available at University Village Copy Store)
Visions Across the Americas (VAA), Warner, Hiliard, Piro
Practical English Handbook (PEH), Watkins and Dillingham
A college dictionary
Two 3.5-in. floppy disks, double-sided, double-density
Journal: a stenographer's notebook
VAX computer username (available with student ID in RB 165)

Course Requirements

	Portion of grade
Portfolio of three essays selected and revised from six required essays	75%
Fifty-minute timed writing	15%
Class participation, journals	10%

You MUST pass the portfolio and the timed writing (at least a C average on each) in order to pass the course and go on to 102.

Class Policies

Attendance: Because the course is conducted in a workshop format, your attendance is vital and mandatory. With this in mind, consider yourselves forewarned: More than *four* absences could result in your failing English 101. If you are absent for any reason, you are responsible for (1) notifying your instructor the day you are absent, and (2) finding out about and making up any missed work the day after you return to class.

Grading

Portfolio: Because this course is structured around a portfolio system, letter grades are not placed on individual essays as they are completed throughout the semester. These essays will be marked S (Satisfactory—would receive a C or better if graded) or U (Unsatisfactory—would receive lower than a C if graded).

Of the six essays written during the semester, you will select three to fully revise and submit for evaluation by at least two other English instructors. NOTE: All drafts of all essays must be included in the portfolio.

The three portfolio essays MUST be judged at C level or better in terms of content, organization, development, mechanics, and appropriate handling of audience and purpose. Half of your portfolio grade will be determined by the final portfolio *product*, and half will be affected by your involvement in the portfolio *process*—completion of all reading and writing assignments leading up to each final paper. This also means that all drafts of all six essays must be turned in on time.

Timed Writing: The timed writing, too, will be evaluated by at least two other English instructors and must receive a grade of C or better.

Late Papers: Everyone receives one act of mercy for late papers (including drafts). After that, 1 percent is subtracted from your portfolio grade for each day any draft or final paper is late. The final portfolio MUST be turned in on December 4—NO EXCEPTIONS.

Plagiarism: Using someone else's ideas is a serious offense, and any act of plagiarism will result in failure of the course.

CLASS SCHEDULE AND ASSIGNMENTS
ENGLISH 101

Remember: Every Monday we will meet in the computer lab unless otherwise noted. Always bring floppy disks and any drafts you are working on at that time.

Note: I reserve the right to alter the following schedule at any time.

Week 1 (August 26–28)

Wed.   Introduction to the course; obtain VAX username and password.
Fri.   Diagnostic essay (in class); read pp. 1–8, 272–275 in VAA.

Week 2 (August 31–September 4)

Mon.   Language pretest in RB 134—bring username and student ID.
Wed.   Discuss readings; read writing history assignment and example in handout packet.
Fri.   Introduction to computer lab; read pp. 8–12, 28–37 in VAA. Rough draft of writing history due Wednesday.

Week 3 (September 7–11)

Mon.   LABOR DAY—NO CLASSES.
Wed.   Bring rough draft of writing history; peer review using editing sheets in handout packet.
Fri.   PAPER 1 DUE; read pp. 39–46 VAA; define *memoir* in journal, and fill out worksheets in handout packet.

Week 4 (September 14–18)

Mon.   COMPUTER LAB; read "The Kitten," "All's Forgiven" (handouts).
Wed.   Discuss readings.
Fri.   Watch movie; rough draft of memoir due Wednesday.

Week 5 (September 21–25)

Mon.   COMPUTER LAB
Wed.   Peer editing using sheets in handout packet.
Fri.   PAPER 2 DUE; read pp. 21–27, 130–133 in VAA; have three tentative topics to discuss Monday.

Week 6　*(September 28–October 2)*

Mon.　COMPUTER LAB; read pp. 246–251 in VAA, and "From Poets in the Kitchen" and "Jeans" (handouts).

Wed.　Discuss readings; rough draft of "Familiar as New" due Friday.

Fri.　Peer editing.

Week 7　*(October 5–9)*

Mon.　COMPUTER LAB; read pp. 270–272 VAA.

Wed.　Peer editing.

Fri.　PAPER 3 DUE; read pp. 308–312, 354–356 VAA.

Week 8　*(October 12–16)*

Mon.　COMPUTER LAB; practice timed writing.

Wed.　Discuss readings; rough draft of letter to editor due Friday.

Fri.　Peer editing.

Week 9　*(October 19–23)*

Mon.　COMPUTER LAB.

Wed.　Peer editing.

Fri.　PAPER 4 DUE; read pp. 72–82 VAA.

Week 10　*(October 26–30)*

Mon.　COMPUTER LAB: MIDTERM TIMED WRITING.

Wed.　Discuss reading; read "Place Observation Report" and "Balinese Cockfight" in handout packet.

Fri.　Discussion; rough draft of ethnographic study due Wednesday.

Week 11　*(November 2–6)*

Mon.　COMPUTER LAB.

Wed.　Peer editing.

Fri.　PAPER 5 DUE; meet in library for library instruction.

Week 12　*(November 9–13)*

Mon.　COMPUTER LAB.

Wed.　Practice timed writing.

Fri.　No class meeting: CONFERENCES.

Week 13 (November 16–20)

Mon.   COMPUTER LAB; PAPER 6 DUE.
Wed.   Practice timed writing.
Fri.   No class meeting: CONFERENCES.

Week 14 (November 23)

Mon.   COMPUTER LAB.

THANKSGIVING BREAK.

Week 15 (November 30–December 4)

Mon.   COMPUTER LAB; practice timed writing.
Wed.   Nuts and bolts review.
Fri.   *PORTFOLIOS DUE; FINAL TIMED WRITING.*

Week 16 (December 7–11)

Mon.   Course evaluations; tying up loose ends.
Wed.   Portfolio evaluation.
Fri.   Portfolio evaluation.

Week 17 (December 14–18)

Tue. Scheduled final exam time—December 15, 9:45–11:45.

SAMPLE SYLLABUS 2

ENGLISH 103
COURSE OVERVIEW

Dr. R. L. Peterson
Semester: Autumn
Office: ENG 254   Office Phone: 555-8588
English Department Office Phone: 555-8580

Course Requirements and Policies

Texts: The Beacon Handbook, Perrin
The Riverside Reader, 4th ed., Trimmer and Hairston

Materials Packet (available at English Department Office,
Room 295)
The Writing Program, 1992–93, BSU English Department
Any good college dictionary (for example, *The American
Heritage Dictionary*)

Materials: You will need at least one 3.5-in. computer disk for computer
lab meetings of this class. You must have a folder with regular, loose-
leaf notebook paper for class notes, exercises, and themes. *NO SPIRAL
NOTEBOOK PAPER MAY BE TURNED IN IN THIS CLASS.* You must write in
blue or black ink. Always bring paper to class because you will
usually be expected to write or take notes.

Assignments: Themes—During this semester you will write and revise
papers as assigned. All themes will be written on white, lined paper,
using every other line. Papers written out of class will be typewritten.
Each theme is to be 400 to 500 words in length (4 to 5 handwritten
pages, depending on your handwriting). In order to pass English 103,
you must write all themes according to announced specifications.

Late Work: Work submitted after the hour in which it is due will be
penalized one letter grade per class meeting that it is late.

Attendance: Attendance at all class meetings is very important. If you
must be absent, call the instructor to obtain assignments in advance
of the absence and to arrange to turn in any work due during your
absence. You can also contact your instructor by leaving a message
at the English Department office (555-8580) or via computer VAX
mail. Otherwise, late assignments will be considered to be late work
(see above).

Three or more absences will adversely affect your course grade. *IN
SHORT, ATTENDANCE IS REQUIRED IN THIS COURSE.*

Course Grades

Course grades are determined as follows:

	Portion of grade
Daily work (including diagnostic writings, drafts, quizzes, peer-editing papers, freewritings, library instruction materials, and so on)	1/6
Narrative-descriptive theme revision	1/6
Comparison-contrast theme revision	1/6
Interview-investigation theme revision	1/3
Argument-research (final) theme revision	1/6

Copies of Themes

Copies of student themes (with names removed) will be used during class discussion. Students will also be required to trade papers for peer-editing exercises. Please be advised that fellow students will read your papers; choose your topics accordingly.

ENGLISH 103/88
COURSE SYLLABUS (AUTUMN)

August

W   26   Course introduction
Draft diagnostic theme

M   31   Introduction to revision

September

W   2   Revise diagnostic theme
Angelou 26, Kovic 34

M   7   LABOR DAY—NO CLASS
Sanders 558

W   9   Introduction to narration
Orwell 43, Bambara 77

M   14   Attend one of the UniverCity lectures on campus

W   16   More narration
Draft narrative theme

M   21   Introduction to peer editing

W   23   Introduction to description
Selzer 132, O'Connor 270

M   28   Narrative-descriptive theme due (written out of class)
Introduction to comparison-contrast
Twain 165, Hall 175

W   30   Comparison-contrast organizational strategies
Winn 188, Walker 209

October

M   5   Draft comparison-contrast paper in class
W   7   Peer editing

M   12   Comparison-contrast revision due (written out of class)
           Introduction to interview
           Mittford 115
W   14   Interview techniques
           Morris, Bell

M   19   Interview paper organization strategies
           Trillin 414, Berkow, McPhee
W   21   Begin interview reports
           Terkel

M   26   Interview reports
W   28   Interview reports

November

M   2   Interview draft due
          Peer editing
W   4   Interview revision due

M   9   Introduction to causal analysis
          Staples 371, Gould 387
W   11   Introduction to argument
           King 460, Quindlen 472

M   16   Argument paper organization strategies
           Sagan 518, Dyson 528
W   18   Private argument draft due
           Incorporating research

M   23   Library instruction

THANKSGIVING BREAK

M   30   Research paper fundamentals

December

W   2   Documenting research
            Stone 477

M   7   Argument-research rough draft due
            Peer editing

W   9   Course evaluation
            All papers must be returned to English Department.

Final exam: argument-research papers due

SAMPLE SYLLABUS 3

COURSE OUTLINE
ENGLISH COMPOSITION II
Vincennes University

Course Books and Materials and Grading

See attached Weekly Assignment Schedule for texts, materials, and grading standards specified by individual instructors.

Organization and Content

Purpose of the Course

Composition II is a continuation of the work started in Composition I to help the student develop his or her ability to think, to organize, and to express his or her thoughts and ideas effectively, both in written and in oral form. It applies the skills developed in English I to a wider range of expository writing, culminating in the preparation of an investigative paper.

Written Work

A minimum of 6,000 words is required, including one investigative paper (between 8 and 12 typed pages), one short documented paper (between 4 and 6 typed pages), and one other documented essay.

Oral Work

One oral presentation is optional.

Procedures

Class will include discussion of textbook models; lectures on techniques involved in the preparation of an investigative paper; introduction to the library as a laboratory; exercises in note taking, documentation of statements, and preparation of outlines and bibliographies; exercises in forming and testing generalizations, evaluating evidence, and recognizing prejudicial devices.

Attendance

Attendance will be taken every class meeting and students are expected to arrive *on time*. A late arrival may be counted absent. The university attendance policy will be strictly followed, and students with excessive absences will be withdrawn from the course.

Plagiarism

Plagiarism is the act of using another person's words and ideas as if they were one's own. Any student who is found to be plagiarizing on a paper or who allows his or her paper to be copied will automatically receive an *F* for that paper and will be reported to the dean of students for disciplinary action.

COMP II: HEW 102	**Dr. Laurel Smith**
Course Evaluation, Procedures	**HUM E-149**
Spring Semester	**Phone: 555-4140, 4512**

Evaluation

HEW 102   100% = 1000 points

Documentation project   15%   (150 points)
    Critique 1
    Critique 2
    Annotated bibliography
Investigative paper   30%   (300 points)
    Rough draft and conference
    Oral report on research
    Final paper (8 to 12 typed pages)

Essays

Argumentation	15%	(150 points)
Exposition	10%	(100 points)
Essay test	10%	(100 points)

Quizzes/participation   10%   (100 points)
    Research quizzes
    Reading quizzes

Directed journal   10%   (100 points)

Specific guidelines for each assignment will be given in class and must be followed. *Minimum standards,* as defined by the English Department at Vincennes University, will be used to evaluate all written work.

Procedures

Class time is used to discuss readings, to plan writing projects, to clarify research and documentation procedures, and to exchange ideas about writing. Students are expected to come to class every day, on time, prepared to participate.

Comp II is a college-level course that further demands that each student use self-discipline and time-management skills to complete assignments. Students must effectively use class time and time out of class to achieve course goals. A missed essay due to an excused absence must be completed *promptly.*

Late papers without an official excuse (approved by the dean) will not be accepted. Questions about missed work and absences need to be discussed with the instructor before or after class (during my office hours)—not during class time.

Missed quizzes may not be made up.

HEW 102: WEEKLY ASSIGNMENT SCHEDULE
Dr. Laurel Smith   Office: HUM E-149
Spring Semester   Phone: 555-4140, 4512

Texts: RP = Coyle, *Research Papers*
        LTL = Keating and Levy, eds., *Lives Through Literature*

Week 1, January 11–15

Topics: Introduction to course
Critical reading

Assignment: LTL   Joan Didion, "Marrying Absurd"
Andrea Lee, "The Wedding"

Week 2, January 18–22

Topics: Myth, fiction, drama
Directed journals

Assignment: LTL   Homer, from "The Odyssey"
Mary W. Freeman, "The Revolt of Mother"
Ibsen, *A Doll House*

Week 3, January 25–29

Topics: Drama and analysis
Documentation and critical writing

Assignment: Ibsen (continued)
RP 183–185

Week 4, February 1–5

Topics: Writing with argumentation, documentation
Proposals for research

Assignment: **Essay 1 due**
RP 49–66, 311–331

Week 5, February 8–12

Topics: Library research, bibliography cards
Assignment: RP 11–18, 27–45

Week 6, February 15–19

Topics: Note taking, critique writing
Assignment: **Tentative bibliography due**
Critique 1 due
RP 77–97

Week 7, February 22–26

Topics: Note taking, interviewing expert resources
Assignment: **Interview questions due**

Week 8, March 1–5

Topics: Note taking, interviewing
Assignment: **Note cards due**
Critique 2 due

Week 9, Midterm Break (March 6–14)

Week 10, March 15–19

Topics: Annotated bibliography
Formal outline
Assignment: RP Chapter 8, 107–123
Annotated bibliography due

Week 11, March 22–26

Topics: Writing the rough draft
Assignment: RP 143–159
Conferences: Outline and rough draft due

Week 12, March 29–April 2

Topics: Rough draft to final form
Assignment: RP 167–178

Week 13, April 5–8

Topics: Oral reports, final drafts
Assignment: RP 119–253
Investigative research paper due: April 8, 4:00 P.M.

Week 14, April 12–16

Topics: Poetry and aesthetics (Theme: Siblings in myth)
Assignment: LTL Grimm Brothers, "Cinderella" (tale)
Bruno Bettelheim, "Cinderella" (essay)
Gwendolyn Brooks, "Sadie and Maud" (poem)
William Wordsworth, "We Are Seven" (poem)
Seamus Heaney, "Mid-Term Break" (poem)
Diane Keatig, "For Summers" (poem)
Susan Fawcett, "The Slow Way to Forgiveness"

Week 15, April 19–23

   Topics: Questions of value, questions of significance
   Assignment: LTL   Alice Munro, "Boys and Girls"
                      James Baldwin, "Sonny's Blues"
                      Edith Wharton, "Roman Fever"
                      Jean Paul Sartre, "The Wall"
         Essay 2 due

Week 16, April 26–30

   Topics: Questions and response
   Assignment: **Essay 3 due (essay test)**

APPENDIX B

A Brief Guide to Houghton Mifflin Composition Texts

RHETORICS/GUIDES TO WRITING

Barnwell/Dees, *The Resourceful Writer*, Third Edition, 1994, 544 pp., paperback. Instructor's Resource Manual.

This accessible text covers longer paragraph and essay writing. It follows a clear progression for developing skills: writing from personal experience, writing in the rhetorical modes, and writing with outside sources. Contains a grammar workbook and a research chapter.

Bazerman, *The Informed Writer: Using Sources in the Disciplines*, Fifth Edition, 1995, 512 pp., paperback. Instructor's Resource Manual.

Emphasizing the close connection between reading and writing, Bazerman provides detailed instruction on how to synthesize and document sources in a variety of disciplines and how to formulate sound, original arguments. Features one-third new readings, expanded use of student writing and examples, and new model papers. Used chiefly in the second-semester, research-oriented composition course.

Hunt, *The Riverside Guide to Writing*, Second Edition, 1994. Long: 704 pp., hardcover. Brief (omits handbook): 576 pp., paperback. Instructor's Guide. Software.

Hunt's distinctive guide helps students write better papers by helping them find a new framework for familiar subjects. Guidance is offered in the major types of college writing: memoir, report, evaluation, proposal, argument, literary paper, and research paper. The book features strong coverage of argument and a rich collection of readings and now presents clearer coverage of the writing process.

Kanar, *The Confident Writer*, 1994, 484 pp., paperback. Instructor's Resource Manual.

Kanar's student-oriented text builds confidence as it builds skills. The book integrates multicultural readings and numerous boxed features (critical thinking, collaborative learning, journal writing, grammar) into clear and seamless chapters.

Keller, *Aims and Options: A Thematic Approach to Writing*, 1995, 480 pp., paperback. Instructor's Resource Manual.

Keller bases his book on Kinneavey's aims of discourse and builds each chapter around a compelling theme carried through in the examples and readings. Includes a variety of readings, a research section, integrated grammar, and coverage of all the rhetorical modes in each chapter.

Rawlins, *The Writer's Way*, Second Edition, 1992, 480 pp., paperback. Instructor's Resource Manual.

Distinguished by its informal, personal tone, this practical rhetoric is based on the "whole language" approach. The new edition features 8 chapters on revision; an anthology of 39 student papers; 16 "writer's workshops"; expanded handbook; and new material on collaborative learning, critical thinking, and word processing.

Trimmer, *Writing with a Purpose*, Eleventh Edition, 1995, 672 pp., hardcover. Instructor's Resource Manual. Instructor's Support Package. Diagnostic Tests. Computerized Diagnostic Tests (IBM). PEER: Practical English Exercises and Review (software) (IBM/MAC).

This comprehensive rhetoric / reader / handbook / research guide emphasizes purpose throughout the writing process. It contains numerous student and professional readings and sequences of writing assignments that move from personal narrative to analysis to argument. This classic text has been perfected over years of classroom use and is a fail-safe rhetoric for new and experienced instructors alike.

READERS

Atwan, *Best American Essays, College Edition*, 1994. Instructor's Resource Manual.

The editor of the widely used *Best American Essays* series here selects compelling essays by today's best writers and organizes them into coherent thematic clusters. This brief and relatively inexpensive book also includes a collection of reflections on the essay itself by various writers and gives several alternate tables of contents (including by rhetorical mode) for flexibility.

Conlin, *Patterns Plus: A Short Prose Reader with Argumentation*, Fifth Edition, 1995, 409 pp., paperback. Instructor's Resource Manual.

An anthology of paragraphs and short essays, arranged by rhetorical strategy, with a chapter on argumentation. Includes a more culturally diverse selection of readings.

Fakundiny, *The Art of the Essay*, 1991, 768, pp., paperback. Instructor's Resource Manual.

86 essays, chronologically arranged, that represent the best in four centuries of the personal essay in English.

Hunt/Perry, *The Dolphin Reader*, Third Edition, 1993, 800 pp., paperback. Instructor's Resource Manual.

Divided into 8 thematic units, the readings (76 essays, 8 short stories, and 1 play) have carefully been selected and arranged to allow "conversations" among multiple viewpoints about universal issues. The units proceed from personal to public concerns, and links among the units have been strengthened. A section of writing assignments draws connections among readings. The Instructor's Resource Manual contains new Style Lessons that help students apply the strategies used by professional writers to their own essays.

Moseley/Harris, *Interactions: A Thematic Reader*, Second Edition, 1994, 544 pp., paperback. Instructor's Resource Manual.

This popular thematic reader is organized around the theme of *self*. Moseley and Harris focus on the connections between reading and writing processes. The new edition contains critical thinking exercises and new collaborative learning activities.

Rico/Mano, *American Mosaic: Multicultural Readings in Context*, Second Edition, 1994, 704 pp., paperback. Instructor's Resource Manual.

This historically based multicultural reader explores the literary and cultural development of ethnic groups in America, spotlighting a particular moment in time (e.g., the Japanese internment, the civil rights movement). The apparatus features an expanded critical thinking focus, and exercises range from journal keeping to collaborative activities to research-based responses.

Roberts/Turgeon, *About Language: A Reader for Writers*, Fourth Edition, 1995, 560 pp., paperback. Instructor's Resource Manual.

Over 70 selections, mostly essays, explore language issues of current and enduring interest. The extensive apparatus supports composition instruction. Revision features about 50 percent new selections.

Schaum/Flanagan, *Gender Images: Readings for Composition*, 1992, 704 pp., paperback. Instructor's Resource Manual.

This thematically organized reader focuses on the timely issue of gender, with a balanced selection of essays, fiction, and poetry by men and women. The apparatus emphasizes critical thinking, rhetorical strategies, and sequential writing assignments. The interdisciplinary theme introduces students to such diverse fields as linguistics, psychology, politics, and sociology.

Smoke, *Making a Difference*, 1994, 454 pp., paperback. Instructor's Resource Manual.

The 43 diverse readings in this collection highlight people who have overcome obstacles and made a difference in their communities. Apparatus encourages collaborative writing and critical thinking and helps connect the readings to the students' own writing. Includes an appendix of organizations and activities to make a difference.

Trimmer/Hairston, *The Riverside Reader*, Fourth Edition, 1993, 704 pp., paperback. Instructor's Resource Manual.

This rhetorically organized collection of 46 essays and 8 short stories emphasizes the connection between the reading and writing processes and presents the modes as ways of thinking and discovering purpose. The Fourth Edition features paired argumentation essays on such issues as race relations and animal rights, and new discussion questions and writing assignments. Half of the selections are new to this edition.

Walker/McClish, *Investigating Arguments: Readings for College Writing*, 1991, 800 pp., paperback. Instructor's Resource Manual.

A chronologically organized anthology of readings spanning a broad historical spectrum from the fifth century B.C. to the present.

Wiener/Bazerman, *Side by Side: A Multicultural Reader*, 1993, 496 pp., paperback. Instructor's Resource Manual.

Includes 60 mainly nonfiction pieces from diverse cultural perspectives. Organized into 6 themes that highlight facets of American society's diversity. Extensive support throughout the text encourages critical thinking, interpretation, and collaborative learning as well as comprehension and vocabulary work.

Zaitchik / Roberts / Zaitchik, *Face to Face: Readings on Confrontation and Accommodation in America*, 1994, 572 pp., paperback. Instructor's Resource Manual.

Face to Face stands apart from other multicultural readers by virtue of its approach, seeing not a melting pot but shifting moments of confrontation and accommodation, and its distinct four-part organization. The selections are exceptionally diverse in genre, historical period, and culture. The apparatus emphasizes critical thinking and connects readings to the writing process.

HANDBOOKS

Bazerman / Wiener, *Writing Skills Handbook*, Third Edition (English Essential Series), 1993, 160 pp., spiralbound. Instructor's Support Package.

Focuses on the most common writing problems, contains no exercises, and is deliberately very brief. Rules and examples are succinct, simple, and largely devoid of grammar terminology. New spiral binding lets the book lie flat for easy use.

Beene / Vande Kopple, *The Riverside Handbook*, 1992, 864 pp., hardcover. Instructor's Resource Manual. Workbook. Writing about Literature booklet. Diagnostic Tests. Computerized ESL-Revision Exercises.

This comprehensive handbook emphasizes the interrelation of reading, writing, and thinking, and the options available to writers. It offers extensive coverage of research and integrates ESL material into the text.

Perrin, *The Beacon Handbook*, Third Edition. Hardcover: 1994, 700 pp. Paper: 1993, 672 pp. Answer Key. The Beacon Workbook. Instructor's Resource Manual for The Beacon Workbook. Writing about Literature booklet (for paperback version). Software: Beacon Exercises and Review and Beacon Editing Exercises (IBM / Mac).

A high-quality, comprehensive, yet low-priced handbook. Features full coverage of writing and research; an emphasis on critical thinking; integrated word-processing boxes; quick reference charts; and succinct, nontechnical explanations. The Third Edition features a new chapter containing practical advice for ESL students. The hardcover version contains a new appendix on writing about literature.

Watkins / Dillingham, *Practical English Handbook*, Ninth Edition, 1992, 508 pp., paperback. Instructor's Annotated Edition. Practical English Workbook. Instructor's Resource Manual for Workbook. Diagnostic Tests. Reference Chart. PEER: Practical English Exercises and Review (software). Comp Diagnostic Tests.

With concise yet comprehensive coverage of the best practices in writing American English, *Practical English Handbook* features expanded treatment of APA documentation with model paper, new student papers, a revised logic section, a new tabbing system, and expanded glossaries.

CRITICAL THINKING

Chaffee, *Thinking Critically*, Fourth Edition, 1994, 640 pp., paperback. Instructor's Resource Manual. Video: Thinking Toward Decisions.

Develops the fundamental thinking skills and attitudes needed for success in academic courses; for effective reading, writing, and speaking; and for competence in solving problems and making informed decisions in life. The Fourth Edition helps students apply critical thinking to career planning and provides many new readings. Used in four principal courses: Critical Thinking, Composition, Reading, and Freshman Seminar.

Rehner, *Practical Strategies for Critical Thinking* (English Essentials Series), 1994, 140 pp., paperback. Instructor's Resource Manual.

This brief text demystifies critical thinking by providing concrete, class-tested strategies and exercises. Includes ten diverse readings that illustrate critical strategies. Divided into three parts: Critical Reading, Critical Thinking, and Critical Writing.

RESEARCH PAPER

Slade / Campbell / Ballou, *Form and Style: Research Papers, Reports, Theses*, Ninth Edition, 1994, 320 pp., spiralbound.

Provides guidelines for writing, documenting, and formatting all kinds of scholarly papers and reports, with 8 3/16" × 11" typed facsimile pages and convenient spiral binding that allows the book to lie flat. Covers MLA, APA, and the brand-new version of *Chicago Manual* documentation styles, now in separate sections marked by clearly visible tabs.

Trimmer, *A Guide to MLA Documentation*, Third Edition (English Essential Series), 1994, 64 pp., paperback.

This brief, portable, accessible guide to MLA documentation style provides the essentials students need, plus a full sample student paper (new topic: "The Recycling Controversy"). Also offers tips on note taking, summarizing, and other writing and research matters, plus an appendix on APA style.

REFERENCE

American Heritage College Dictionary, Third Edition, 1993, 1,568 pp., hardcover, thumb-indexed.

Contains more than 200,000 definitions. Special features include usage notes, a concise manual of style, over 3,000 illustrations, and a restored and improved appendix of Indo-European roots. Available at a special low price when adopted in a shrink-wrapped package with any Houghton Mifflin college text. Also available in a Concise version (briefer, more portable, and less expensive).

Roget's II: The New Thesaurus, Expanded Edition, 1988, 1,152 pp., hardcover.

More than 20,700 entry words are listed alphabetically with clear definitions and illustrative examples. Synonyms are grouped by precise meanings.

Index